THE TRAVELLER'S
COMPANION

Edited by Georgina Newbery
and Rhiannon Guy

A THINK BOOK FOR

ROBSON BOOKS

The Cook's Companion
Edited by Jo Swinnerton
ISBN 1-86105-772-5

The Gardener's Companion
Edited by Vicky Bamforth
ISBN 1-86105-771-7

The Wildlife Companion
Edited by Malcolm Tait and Olive Tayler
ISBN 1-86105-770-9

SERIES EDITORS

Malcolm Tait and Emma Jones

*It is good to have an end to journey towards,
but it is the journey that matters in the end.*

Ursula K LeGuin

THINK

A Think Book
for Robson Books

First published in Great Britain in 2004 by
Robson Books
The Chrysalis Building, Bramley Road, London W10 6SP

An imprint of **Chrysalis** Books Group plc

Edited by Georgina Newbery and Rhiannon Guy
The Companion team: Vicky Bamforth, Sarah Bove, James Collins,
Harry Glass, Annabel Holmes, Emma Jones, Lou Millward Tait
and Malcolm Tait

Think Publishing
The Pall Mall Deposit
124-128 Barlby Road, London W10 6BL
www.thinkpublishing.co.uk

ISBN 1-86105-773-3

Printed and bound by Clays Ltd, Bungay, Suffolk NR35 1ED

*If you actually look like your passport photo,
you aren't well enough to travel.*

Sir Vivian Fuchs

GLOBAL THANKS

This book would not have been possible without the research, ideas, and dogged support of:

Sam Green-Armytage, Gemma Barnett,
Katie Braun, Ollie and Jules Campbell, Jessica Cardenas,
Gemma Clunie, Ed Dowding, Katherine Lawrey,
Naomi Pollard, Nick Smith,
Angharad, Douglas and Kay Guy,
Toby Wagstaff and Mike Woods.

INTRODUCTION

This is the book for anyone who has been bitten by the travel bug, seized by wanderlust or trotted the globe. If you are embarking on your own great odyssey or looking back fondly on your travelling days from your armchair this is a backpack buddy you can't be without.

It won't tell you anything about the nightlife in New Zealand, when the museums open in Moscow, or the best beds in Bogota. But it will keep you company wherever you are with amusing anecdotes, surprising snippets and treasured travel tips.

Even if your body can't wander, set your mind free to ponder some of the burning questions facing all travellers. Where exactly is the safest place to sit on an aeroplane? What is the strangest thing someone has stolen from a hotel room? Who mistook Hitler for a doorman? Why is an elephant struggling with the Euro? And where on earth is the world's largest peanut?

Whether you are waiting for a bus, whiling away the evening after some energetic sightseeing, or just trying to impress your fellow wayfarers with your travel trivia, *The Traveller's Companion* is for you. Enjoy the journey.

Rhiannon Guy, Editor

GIVE THE WORLD A BREAK

Avoid disturbing traditional festivities

Refrain from intruding on special occasions, especially if not accompanied by a guide who can act as an intermediary on your behalf.

Choose trains over planes

Planes are the fastest-growing contributors to global warming. Train rides are not only environmentally friendlier, they also provide a more interesting journey.

Responsible photography

Always ask people before taking their photos, respect their answer and keep your word if you promise to send them a copy. Do not use flash in places where it could damage delicate surfaces.

Local lingo

Try to learn several words in the local language to show your interest in the place and facilitate your welcome.

Respect the local dress code

When in Rome do as the Romans; respect the local clothing etiquette and forsake your bikini, tank tops or shorts when you are in a religious or traditional area.

BIG BANG

It's accepted that different countries have different customs. And it's perhaps fair to say that a cabbie in Scotland can expect a bit of light banter with passengers and possibly a small tip, especially if the passengers in question are newly-weds in good cheer. Jan Wawryluk was surprised, though, when just such a couple who he was driving to Edinburgh airport offered him a hand grenade for his troubles. Explanation? It was a relic from World War I, which they wouldn't be allowed to take on their flight.

After picking up a few more fares with this alarming antique in his cab, Mr Wawryluk decided to hand it in to police, who promptly called in the bomb disposal squad and sent a worldwide alert out to trace the couple who had given the explosive tip.

QUOTE UNQUOTE

When you travel, remember that a foreign country is not designed to make you comfortable. It is designed to make its own people comfortable.
CLIFTON FADIMAN, writer and critic

Number, in millions, of chocolate mints Carnival Cruise Lines put on their guests' pillows in an average year

FANTASTIC FESTIVITIES

The Bun Festival, Hong Kong, *May*

The Taoist Cheung Chau Bun Festival is one of Hong Kong's liveliest and most bizarre festivities. Every May for four days, huge bamboo towers are built and covered in buns. The festival used to involve people scaling the towers to retrieve the buns for good luck, but now people just turn up to look at the spectacular towering buns. On the third day of the festival, children are carried through the streets on poles and appear to float over the heads of the crowds. Other attractions include stilt walkers and people dressed as legendary characters.

THE DESTINATION TOP 10

Country	International visitors (in 2001)
France	76,500,000
Spain	49,500,000
USA	45,500,000
Italy	39,000,000
China	33,200,000
UK	23,400,000
Russia	21,200,000
Mexico	19,800,000
Canada	19,700,000
Austria	18,200,000

G'DAY MATE

A trip down under turned from a sunny delight into a chilly fright for two teenagers from London in 2002. The pair had been looking forward to an antipodean adventure and had booked a holiday over the internet to Sydney, Australia. Or so they thought. They had actually booked a holiday to Sydney, Canada.

Apparently not noticing that all their fellow passengers were wrapped up against the impending chill, nor that they were flying over the Atlantic, it was not until the couple actually arrived in Nova Scotia that they realised the full extent of their mistake. Well, not quite: 'we thought we were stopping for a stopover' said Raeoul Sebastian.

The couple travelled back to the UK as soon as they could and presumably vowed to pay more attention to the country they were going to next time.

WHY FLAGS AREN'T IN BLACK AND WHITE

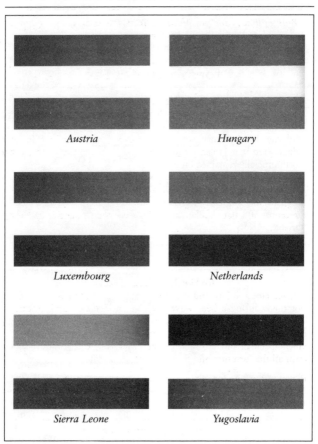

Austria

Hungary

Luxembourg

Netherlands

Sierra Leone

Yugoslavia

TRAVEL TEASERS

My first is in Ireland but never in Wales
My second's in engine but never in sails
My third is in Denmark but never in Greece
My fourth is in Paris and also in Nice
My fifth is in transport and also in fast
My whole is a nation that has a rich past
Answer on page 153

12 *Average distance, in thousands of kilometres, travelled by the world
population in one year*

QUOTE UNQUOTE

Both optimists and pessimists contribute to society. The optimist
invents the aeroplane, the pessimist the parachute.
GEORGE BERNARD SHAW, playwright

TOPSY TURVY GLOBE

So who was it who decided to put the North at the top of all the maps?
And why? Step forward Ptolemy, famous 2nd-century Greek
astronomer and a man very much ahead of his time. However, it wasn't
until the 16th century when map-maker extraordinaire Mercator
rediscovered that Ptolemy had placed North at the top of maps that
North officially remained on top.

During the 1,300-year gap, religious interests dictated where the top of
the globe was. For early Christians, it was the East, with Jerusalem in
the centre of a flat circular map. This gave rise to the concept of the
'Orient'.

DISTINCTIVE DWELLINGS

Ice Hotel, Lapland, Sweden
The Ice Hotel in Lapland is forever changing. And make sure you're
not there during a heat wave. This ice palace was first created in
1990, and every November a team of sculptors and architects lovingly
re-crafts the large igloo hotel, complete with sparkling ballrooms,
cinema, chapel and 'Absolut Ice Bar'. Every single bedroom is unique
with all the furniture and fittings made from ice.

If you're not one for winter and hate the cold, don't worry: like the
local Sami people, you'll sleep on a block of ice covered in cosy
reindeer pelts.

GRAND TOURING

If you'd been a nobleman in the 18th century you'd have completed
(and in some cases perhaps started) your education with a period of
travel around Europe known as a 'Grand Tour'. The length of your trip
would depend on the size of your wallet, so anything from a few
months to eight years was acceptable. The fashionable dots on the map
you and your entourage had to try and join up were Venice, Naples,
Sicily and Rome. You were also expected to return with a collection of
bona fide classical antiquities to show off (a sort of Continental
supermarket sweep), although many adventurers just returned with
new, more virulent strains of venereal disease.

Krung thep mahanakhon bovorn ratanakosin mahintharayutthaya mahadilok pop noparatratchathani burirom udomratchanivetmahasathan amornpiman avatarnsathit sakkathattiyavisnukarmprasit (167 letters)
This poetic name is usually abbreviated to 'Krung Thep', the City of Angels, referring to Bangkok, Thailand's capital.

Taumatawhakatangihangakoauauotamateaturipukakapikimaungah oronukupokaiwhenuakitinatahu (85 letters)
'The place where Tamatea, the man with the big knees, who slid, climbed and swallowed mountains, known as land-eater, played on the flute to his loved one' is the Maori name of a hill in New Zealand.

Gorsafawddachaidraigddaneddogleddollonpenrhynareurdraethcere digion (67 letters)
The Fairbourne Steam Railway in North Wales invented this name to rival their more famous Welsh counterpart below. It translates to 'The Mawddach station and its dragon teeth at the Northern Penrhyn Road on the golden beach of Cardigan Bay'.

Llanfairpwllgwyngyllgogerychwyrndrobwll-llantysiliogogogoch (58 letters)
This train station's official name 'St Mary's Church in the hollow of the white hazel near to the rapid whirlpool of the church of St Tysilo near the Red Cave' was apparently a prank, humorously thought up by a local tailor.

El Pueblo de Nuestra Senora la Reina de los Angeles de la Porciunucula (57 letters)
Who would have thought 'The town of Our Lady the Queen of the Angels of the Little Portion' is the original name of Los Angeles, once the site of a Franciscan mission?

Chargoggagoggmanchaugagoggchaubunagungamaug (43 letters)
This is the longest place name in the USA and means 'You fish on your side, I'll fish on mine, and no one fishes in the middle' in Nipmuck Indian. It was concocted in the 1920s by the editor of the *Webster Times*, Massachusetts, and is based on a shorter version of a nearby lake.

Lower North Branch Little Southwest Miramichi (40 letters)
A somewhat convoluted name of a river in New Brunswick, which happens to be Canada's longest place name.

14 *Percentage of new entries in the 2004* Who's Who, *who list their top recreation as 'travel'*

TAXI TRAVELLER LOSES HER WAY

The New World, full of the American dream, vast open spaces with breathtaking scenery and thriving cities. A must see on many a traveller's list. But how to get around? Plane, train or automobile? One women opted for automobile. But not just any car. Patricia Agness has no driving licence but she hates buses and planes. So, the only option seemed to be to get a cab. For 10,000 miles. The 55-year-old negotiated a one-dollar-a-mile fare and set off from her Florida home. Two drivers worked in eight hour shifts to try and complete the trip, which would take in 30 cities and finish in Alaska. However, the taxi drivers only made it to California before deciding they'd had enough. The sleep-deprived pair were replaced by a Californian cab driver after 2,500 miles and the journey went on. But not for that long. A commotion in a California hotel led to Agness being arrested and held for psychiatric tests: she had insisted on staying in the hotel's reception, rather than in a room.

LANGUAGES OFFICIALLY SPOKEN IN THE MOST COUNTRIES

	Number of countries
1. English	57
2. French	33
3. Arabic	23
4. Spanish	21
5. Portuguese	7
6= Dutch	5
6= German	5
8= Chinese (Mandarin)	3
8= Danish	3
8= Italian	3
8= Malay	3

QUIZ HIGH-FLYERS

If you're bored and travelling through Singapore's Changi airport, don't fret, for you can take part in a Civil Aviation Authority daily quiz show. This 25-minute diversion, hosted by professional actors, runs 12 times a day and has so far attracted 4,000 game players and crowds of up to a 100 curious onlookers. It's time well spent as the winners get shopping vouchers that they can then spend in the airport before boarding their plane.

ANOTHER SIDE TO THE COINS

When 12 countries switched to the Euro in 2002 it was hoped that, among other things, it would make life easier for tourists travelling between the countries. Perhaps it did.

But however many convergence tests were met by members, there remained one or two large problems when it came to monetary union. One of the most substantial lives in Lisbon Zoo and goes by the name of Jonas. Jonas is a five-tonne African bull elephant who once earned his keep accepting escudos from tourists, ringing a bell for them and hence being fed snacks. His livelihood was threatened when travellers began handing him strange coinage which didn't meet the simple criteria he had been taught: don't accept anything under 20 escudos. His keepers had to retrain him to keep him up with the times, possibly bringing into being the world's first crash course in elementary economics for elephants.

QUOTE UNQUOTE

Travel is the most primitive of pleasures. There is no greater bore than the travel bore. We do not in the least want to hear what he has seen in Hong Kong.
VITA SACKVILLE-WEST, writer

TRAVELLING CIRCUS

Large waterfalls constitute some of the most popular tourist attractions in the world, but some people are not content just to take a few snaps for their albums. Since 1901, 15 daredevils are thought to have gone over Niagara Falls (on the Canadian side) using barrels wrapped with inner tubes, kayaks and other contraptions, of which only 10 survived.

In 1960, a seven-year-old boy survived, wearing just an inflatable ring, when he went over as a result of a boating accident. And in 2003, Kirk Jones became the first man to survive the 180-ft drop without any device when he jumped in 'on impulse', although his mother later said the Falls had intrigued her son for years. He compared going over to 'being in a giant tunnel, going straight down, surrounded by water', which is hardly surprising: water goes over the Falls at a rate of 150,000 gallons to the second.

After his jump, Kirk faced a fine of around US$7,600, but was immediately recruited as the 'world's greatest stunt man' by the touring Toby Tyler Circus.

THE ISOLATION INDEX

The UN Isolation Index is calculated by adding together the square roots of the distances to the nearest island, group of islands and continent. For example, Easter Island is situated 2,000 miles from the nearest populated areas of Tahiti and Chile.

EAT ME

Quick, get a pen and paper! Early in 2004, *Zoo Weekly* ran a competition offering a jungle holiday with a tribe of cannibals. Interesting idea. The 'winner' would be whisked off (not up) to the Baliem Valley in Papua New Guinea to spend two weeks (if all went well) with the Korowai tribe, who sport tusks in their noses and piercings, wear nothing but long penis gourds... and eat people.

On the up side, the lucky person would be accompanied by a Mr Barker, who has known the tribe for years. On the downside, they would be travelling without maps or phones. But, Mr Barker was very reassuring on the subject: 'It should be OK. The really bad ones are the Korowai's neighbours, the Asmat, and they haven't eaten a Westerner for 40 years,' he said. Well, that's alright then.

Entrants had to write 25 words or less saying why they should go. Funnily enough only two words leap to mind.

A FIVE-STAR ORGY

They say any publicity is good publicity, but when the *People's Daily* in Zhuhai, China reported an orgy at a five-star hotel involving 400 Japanese tourists and 500 prostitutes, that certainly wasn't the case. Although many would argue that the episode would have attracted more customers than it would lose, the authorities swiftly closed the hotel.

INTERMINABLE TERMINALS

Think you've waited a long time to catch a flight? Or have you sat for hours on the runway wondering whether the pilot isn't just doing his duty-free shopping? Well, spare a thought for Merhan Karimi Nasseri. He has been waiting at Paris Charles de Gaulle for 10 years – but he's not waiting to check in, he's waiting to check out.

An Iranian exile expelled for his political beliefs, he was hopping from city to city in Europe searching for relatives when a trap of bureaucracy snapped shut on him.

He had applied and was awarded political asylum, but in 1988, his refugee papers were stolen and he was returned from London to France when he arrived without a passport. The courts determined that he had entered the airport legally as a refugee and therefore could not be expelled from it, but the French government refused to allow him out onto French turf and he has been there ever since.

His clothes are clean, his moustache trimmed and his blazer hangs from an airport cart. Staff call him 'Alfred', and he reads a lot. He occasionally walks to the terminal doors, waits for them to open, and inhales the fresh air as it wafts in, but he never steps outside. He even gets his post sent there.

'He's a part of the airport', said the manager of one of the airport bars. A Lufthansa clerk added: 'That's his table, his chair, his place. He's one of us.'

Pray you never hear those words piped through the speaker.

QUOTE UNQUOTE

All who wander are not lost.
JRR TOLKIEN, creator of Middle Earth

FANTASTIC FESTIVITIES

Burial of the Sardine, Tenerife, Canary Islands, Spain, *February*
This annual festival takes place on Carnival Tuesday (usually the end of February) in several villages around the island. The festivities in Santa Cruz, for example, follow the slow-moving 'death' procession of a huge sardine (made from cloth) mounted on a throne. Its arrival, accompanied by men dressed as pregnant women and wailing widows, at the Plaza Europa is greeted by an enormous firework display with dancing in the street and the laying to rest of the celebrated sardine.

Belize – a country east of Guatemala in the Caribbean; formerly British Honduras

Benin – a country in western Africa; formerly Dahomey

Botswana – a country in south-central Africa; formerly Bechuanaland

Cambodia – a country in south-east Asia on the Gulf of Thailand; formerly Khmer Republic

Djibouti – a country in eastern Africa; formerly Afars and Issas

Ethiopia – a country in north-east Africa; formerly Abyssinia

Greece – a country in south-east Europe, with many islands; formerly Hellas

Lesotho – a country in southern Africa; formerly Basutoland

Malawi – a country in south-east Africa, east of Zambia; formerly Nyasaland

Nauru – an island country in the Pacific, south of the equator and west of Kiribati; formerly Pleasant Island

Sri Lanka – an island country in the Indian Ocean off south-east India; formerly Ceylon

Surinam – a country on the coast of South America; formerly Dutch Guiana

Taiwan – an island country off the south-east coast of China in the South China Sea; formerly Formosa

Thailand – a country in south-east Asia on the Gulf of Thailand; formerly Siam

Tuvalu – an island country in the western Pacific off Fiji; formerly Ellice Islands

United Arab Emirates – a country in eastern Arabia; formerly Trucial Oman

Vanuatu – an island country in the southern Pacific; formerly New Hebrides

Zimbabwe – a country in southern Africa; formerly Rhodesia

THE HITCHER

Abraham Lincoln always had a way with words. On one long walking journey, he hailed a stranger who was driving in his direction and asked if he would take his overcoat into town. The man agreed, but asked how Mr Lincoln expected to get it back: 'Oh, very easily,' came the reply, 'I intend to remain in it.'

OLD POSTER, NEW CAPTION

*As he gazed out from the unmoving trolley, Josiah began to
recollect some vague phrase involving the words 'cart',
'before' and 'horse'.*

QUOTE UNQUOTE

*The use of travelling is to regulate imagination by reality,
and instead of thinking how things might be,
to see them as they are.*
SAMUEL JOHNSON, writer

WHOM WAS THAT?

Enjoyment, relaxation and restlessness: these are just some of the
reasons why we travel, but for Edward de Vere, the Earl of Oxford,
his journey to the continent in the 1550s was prompted by a rather
different motivation. The well-known wit, poet, patron of the theatre
and favourite in the court of Queen Elizabeth, had 'accidentally let
one off' when bowing low to her majesty. After seven years of
embarrassment-fuelled journeying, he arrived home to be greeted by
the Queen's words: 'Really my Lord, I had forgotten the fart'.

ARSE!

If you want to attract tourists, you must learn how they think.
When the company which ran the Peak Cavern in Derbyshire
wanted to whip up more tourism to their caves following the Foot
and Mouth crisis it renamed the site to its original title: Devil's Arse.
The result? A 30% increase in visitors.

Acapulco

Ingredients: 2 measures white rum, 1/2 measure triple sec, 1/2 measure lime juice, 1 tsp sugar syrup and 1 egg white.

Shake the rum, triple sec, lime juice and sugar syrup over cracked ice. Add the egg white and shake again. Serve in a chilled glass and decorate with a sprig of mint.

American Rose

Ingredients: 1 and 1/2 measures brandy, 1 tsp grenadine, 1/2 measure Pernod, half a fresh peach (peeled) and sparkling wine.

Blend the brandy, grenadine, Pernod and fresh peach together. Strain into a chilled wine glass and top up with sparkling wine. Garnish with fresh peach.

Blue Hawaii

Ingredients: 1 and 1/2 measures of white rum, 1/2 measure of dark rum, 1/2 measure of blue curacao, 3 measures of pineapple juice and 1 measure of coconut cream.

Shake the ingredients over cracked ice and serve in a chilled glass.

Cuba Libre

Ingredients: 2 measures of white rum and cola to top up.

Half fill a glass with cracked ice cubes. Pour the rum over the ice and top up with cola. Stir gently to mix, add a splash of lime juice and decorate with wedge of lime.

French 75

Ingredients: 2 measures of brandy, 1 measure of lemon juice, 1 tsp of sugar syrup and chilled champagne to top up.

Shake the brandy, lemon juice and sugar syrup over cracked ice. Top up with champagne and decorate with a twist of lemon.

Italian Margarita

Ingredients: 1 measure of amaretto, 1/2 measure of cointreau, 1/2 measure of tequila and 2 measures of lime juice.

Blend with ice and serve in a salt-rimmed glass, garnish with a wedge of lime.

Long Island Iced Tea

Ingredients: 2 measures of vodka, 1 measure of gin, 1 measure of tequila, 1 measure of white rum, 1/2 measure of triple sec, cola and a dash each of lemon and lime juice and sugar syrup.

Shake all the ingredients over cracked ice, reserving the cola to top up in a high-ball glass before serving. Decorate with a wedge of lemon or lime.

Mexican Grasshopper

Ingredients: 1 measure each of kahlua, white crème de caçao and cream.

Shake over cracked ice and strain into a chilled cocktail flute.

Moscow Mule

Ingredients: 2 measures of vodka, 1 measure of lime juice and ginger beer to top up.

Shake the vodka and lime juice over cracked ice. Pour into a glass, top up with ginger beer and decorate with a wedge of lime.

Around the World

Ingredients: 1 measure of gin, 1 measure of crème de menthe and 2 measures of pineapple juice.

Shake all the ingredients over cracked ice and pour into a chilled glass.

OO-AH, IT'S THE ONLY WAY TO TRAVEL

Three retired British tractor fanatics are planning on travelling around the world in vintage tractors. The tractors' centenary falls in 2004 and the trio feel it is a fitting way to celebrate the anniversary. The route will cover five continents and go through 34 countries. The group are planning to cover approximately 100 miles a day so they can maintain a steady pace, meaning their journey should take them about two years. The men are rebuilding classic tractors for their journey, which now looks like it will start in 2005.

THE SIGNS AREN'T GOOD

Detour sign in Kyushu, Japan:
Stop: Drive sideways.

From a Japanese information booklet about using a hotel air conditioner:
Cooles and Heates: If you want just condition of warm in your room, please control yourself.

From a brochure of a car rental firm in Tokyo:
When passenger of foot heave in sight, tootle the horn. Trumpet him melodiously at first, but if he still obstacles your passage then tootle him with vigour.

Two signs from a Majorcan shop entrance:
English well talking.
Here speeching American.

In a Hong Kong supermarket:
For your convenience, we recommend courageous, efficient self-service.

In an Acapulco hotel:
The manager has personally passed all the water served here.

Copenhagen airline:
We take your bags and send them in all directions.

MESSAGE IN A BOTTLE

There are various ways of finding yourself a date these days, but if you really want to give yourself the best chance of finding Mr (or Mrs) Right, then there is no better method than scrawling a note, putting it in a plastic bottle and throwing it in the sea.

Or so thought Brenda Houston, a boat decorator, who threw this message from a cruise liner off southern Spain: 'I travel a lot on the sea. Tell me what you do in your life. Write to me.'

It took a few months, but eventually she got a bite. A fireman named Christian Jannussi found the bottle in the waters of the Méjean not far from his native Marseilles, and after three years of correspondence they fell in love.

GROUND CONTROL TO MAJOR TOM, DICK AND HARRY

On 28 April 2001, US multi-millionaire Dennis Tito became the world's first space tourist after paying US$20 million for a week's board and lodging on the International Space Station.

Mark Shuttleworth from South Africa went on the same extra-terrestrial cruise in April the following year, and Lance Bass of group N'Sync was planning on being the third, but the Russians stopped his training when he couldn't come up with the cash.

Now the race is on between private companies to tap into the market; after all, where better for a family holiday than space, where no-one can hear you scream?

A US$10 million 'X Prize' awaits the first private company to develop a reusable launch vehicle (RLV) capable of carrying the general public into space. The prize was set up in May 1996 to promote commercial human space flight and is a continuation of the early 20th century competitions that jump-started the aviation industry (Charles Lindbergh's grandson Eric is one of the prize's sponsors). There are 25 registered groups from seven countries currently competing.

It all comes down to money: it currently costs US$10,000 to get one pound (0.45kg) of passenger weight into the Earth's orbit. The new space planes will need to reduce this to US$1,000 per pound, if they are to bring the ticket within reach of even the biggest of the big spenders.

But, it is within sight: a 1998 NASA report suggests that improvements in technology could push fares as low as US$50,000, and possibly down to US$10,000 a decade later. And with a ticket price of US$50,000, there could be up to 500,000 passengers flying into space each year.

WORLD MUSIC

I Left My Heart in San Francisco – Tony Bennett
Copacabana – Barry Manilow
Vienna – Ultravox
New York, New York– Frank Sinatra
I Love Paris – Frank Sinatra
Barcelona – Freddie Mercury with Montserrat Caballe
One Night in Bangkok – Murray Head
Tulips from Amsterdam – Max Bygraves
On an Evening in Roma – Dean Martin

TAG TOTING

Most people collect postcards or stamps. But not 14-year-old Raghav Somani from India. He has the world's largest collection of airline luggage tags. In fact, he has amassed a total of 469 of them. His collection includes tags made of leather and metal and even some special edition tags that were issued for the delegates of the 1992 US Republican convention by Continental Airlines.

A LOAD OF HOT AIR

Archimedes worked out the principles of buoyancy more than 2,000 years ago, and may well have conceived of flying machines, but it was Joseph and Etienne de Montgolfier who invented the first hot-air balloon. The brothers were working in the family paper factory at Annonay, near Lyon in France at the time. They noticed that a shirt drying above the fire was rising and that scraps of paper put in the fireplace flew out of the chimney, and they began experimenting with paper vessels elevated by hot air.

On 4 April 1783, their first balloon, made from fabric coated with alum and paper, flew unmanned for nearly two kilometres at a height of two metres. It was powered by burning straw, manure and other materials in an attached fire pit. On 19 September, a sheep, a duck and a rooster became the first balloon passengers in another Montgolfier design; this time in the presence of Louis XVI at Versailles. The intrepid animals flew for eight minutes at a height of 500m before landing safely in the forests of Vaucresson three kilometres away. Whether they escaped or not is unclear.

Two months later, on 21 November, the Marquis François d'Arlandes and Jean Pilâtre de Rozier became the first humans to fly in an untethered balloon. They rose to 90m, took their hats off to the delighted crowds below, and then rose to 900m before touching back down.

DISTINCTIVE DWELLINGS

Madonna Inn, California, USA

Kitsch doesn't even cover this themed hotel. Over 40 years ago, when themed rooms were something of a novelty, the Madonna Inn decided to make every one of its 109 rooms unique. Some of the options include a cave room, a cabin room, a lace room and a leather room. But even if the interior isn't to your liking, the location will be: the rooms overlook the Pacific coast between San Francisco and Los Angeles.

TRAVEL TEASERS

Where in the US:
M
TANA
Answer on page 153

WANDERLUST – PRE-1300 AD STYLE

The ancient Greek, Scylax of Carryanda explored the Middle East in the 6th century BC. He was sent by the Emperor Darius of Persia who had ideas of conquering India.

An ancient Egyptian, Hannu, made the first self-recorded exploring expedition. He sailed down the Red Sea and explored the south-eastern areas of the Arabian peninsula around 2750 BC. He also went to Ethiopia and Somalia, returning to Egypt with souvenirs that included the spice myrrh before putting his story down in stone.

Second-century BC Chinese explorer Zhang Quian travelled to the Steppes of central Asia during the Han Dynasty at a time when Emperor Han Wudi was looking to open trade relations with his distant neighbours. On his way to visit the Yueh-chih tribe, Quian was imprisoned by the nomadic Hsiung-nu (the Huns) who kept him locked up for 10 years before he managed to escape and continue the remaining 2,000 miles of his journey. His travels helped open up the beginnings of the Silk Road.

Intrepid Eric the Red (the settler of Greenland) had an equally intrepid son, Leif Eriksson who is credited with being the first European to land on Newfoundland – around the year 1000 AD.

St Brendan, also 'Brendan the Gold' and 'Brendan the Voyager' (484–c578) was an Irish abbot, monastery founder, and legendary sea voyager. It's certain he sailed as far as the Hebrides, but he may even have got as far as the Canary Islands and the Azores.

Marco Polo (1254–1324) famously crossed Asia to China to visit the Kublai Khan in Beijing. Polo's written accounts of his travels are the first Western record of coal, porcelain, gunpowder, printing, paper money and silk.

GET YOUR COAT

The term 'erotodromomania' describes the abnormal impulse to travel to escape unwanted sexual situations, which perhaps explains the concept of gap years, or at least returning from them.

THE SIGNS AREN'T GOOD

In a Japanese hotel:
You are invited to take advantage of the chambermaid.

On the menu of a Polish hotel:
Salad a firm's own make; limpid red beet soup with cheesy dumplings in the form of a finger; roasted duck let loose; beef rashers beaten up in the country people's fashion.

On the menu of a Swiss restaurant:
Our wines leave you nothing to hope for.

In an Austrian hotel catering to skiers:
Not to perambulate the corridors in the hours of repose in the boots of ascension.

In a Bangkok dry-cleaner:
Drop your trousers here for best results.

Outside a Hong Kong tailor shop:
Ladies may have a fit upstairs.

In the lobby of a Moscow hotel across from a Russian Orthodox monastery:
You are welcome to visit the cemetery where famous Russian and Soviet composers, artists, and writers are buried daily except Thursday.

QUOTE UNQUOTE

The roads are steep and dangerous, the cold wind is extremely biting, and frequently fierce dragons impede and molest travellers with their inflictions. Those who travel this road should not wear red garments nor carry loud-sounding calabashes.
HSUAN TSANG, 7th century Chinese traveller

SOUL ASYLUM

Reality TV shows are some of the most-watched programmes on television, and now a Belgian asylum centre has decided to take the format and turn it, naturally, to tourism. The idea? Two weeks in a refugee camp. Participants will share space with 300 asylum seekers in the 'De Passage' centre in Westende being fed basic meals with only water to drink.

26 *Percentage of people who would be prepared to travel anywhere in the world for an operation funded by the NHS to get quicker treatment*

MEET THE NEIGHBOURS

1. **China** (15 neighbours)
Afghanistan, Bhutan, India, Kazakhstan, Kyrgyzstan, Laos, Macau, Mongolia, Myanmar, Nepal, North Korea, Pakistan, Russia, Tajikistan, Vietnam

2. **Russia** (14 neighbours)
China, North Korea, Mongolia, Azerbaijan, Belarus, Estonia, Finland, Georgia, Kazakhstan, Latvia, Lithuania, Norway, Poland, Ukraine

3. **Brazil** (10 neighbours)
Argentina, Bolivia, Colombia, French Guiana, Guyana, Paraguay, Peru, Surinam, Uruguay, Venezuela

4= **Democratic Republic of the Congo** (9 neighbours)
Angola, Burundi, Central African Republic, Congo, Rwanda, Sudan, Tanzania, Uganda, Zambia

4= **Germany** (9 neighbours)
Austria, Belgium, Czech Republic, Denmark, France, Luxembourg, Netherlands, Poland, Switzerland

4= **Sudan** (9 neighbours)
Central African Republic, Chad, Democratic Republic of the Congo, Egypt, Eritrea, Ethiopia, Kenya, Libya, Uganda

7= **Austria** (8 neighbours)
Czech Republic, Germany, Hungary, Italy, Liechtenstein, Slovakia, Slovenia, Switzerland

7= **France** (8 neighbours)
Andorra, Belgium, Germany, Italy, Luxembourg, Monaco, Spain, Switzerland

7= **Turkey** (8 neighbours)
Armenia, Azerbaijan, Bulgaria, Georgia, Greece, Iran, Iraq, Syria

10= **Mali** (7 neighbours)
Algeria, Burkina Faso, Côte d'Ivoire, Guinea, Mauritania, Niger, Senegal

10= **Niger** (7 neighbours)
Algeria, Benin, Burkina Faso, Chad, Libya, Mali, Nigeria

10= **Saudi Arabia** (7 neighbours)
Iraq, Jordan, Kuwait, Oman, Qatar, UAE, Yemen

10= **Tanzania** (7 neighbours)
Burundi, Kenya, Malawi, Mozambique, Rwanda, Uganda, Zambia

10= **Ukraine** (7 neighbours)
Belarus, Hungary, Moldova, Poland, Romania, Russia, Slovakia

10= **Zambia** (7 neighbours)
Angola, Democratic Republic of the Congo, Malawi, Mozambique, Namibia, Tanzania, Zimbabwe

The largest landlocked country is Kazakhstan (1,049,156 square miles). Its neighbours are China, Kyrgyzstan, Turkmenistan, Russia and Uzbekistan.

GIVE THE WORLD A BREAK

Preserve coral reefs
As a result of tourism and pollutants, 27% of coral reefs, the most biodiverse of marine eco-systems, have been destroyed. Be a responsible tourist and refrain from touching, anchoring on or retrieving pieces of coral reefs.

Don't stand out
To avoid attracting thieves and cultural segregation, be discrete and don't flash expensive personal belongings.

Misconceptions of time
Time is relative, so relax; don't count on other cultures to be punctual as they often do not share our fixed, mathematical notion of time.

Verify policy statements
Enquire about your tour opera-tor's responsible-tourism policies, such as local and fair employment schemes, and report any discrep-ancies you have encountered to tourism authorities.

Avoid golfing holidays
Golfing holidays are extremely damaging to local communities and the environment. On average, one golf course necessitates 1,500kg of pesticides per year, and can consume as much water as 60,000 villagers.

ST EDMUNDS, ETHIOPIA?

When travelling abroad, it's quite likely you'll find an English newspaper to read on the flight back, but how about a book about your own home town? Frank Warby was in Addis Ababa airport when he spotted a guidebook not of Europe nor Britain, but of Bury St Edmunds. Perhaps the shop owner had mistaken it for a religious tale. The copy was 32 years old and included completely out-of-date pictures of the town and plans for a 'new' hospital which was actually completed in 1972.

LIFE QUESTIONS...

It's the news many people have been longing to hear: being lazy is good for you. German professor Peter Axt believes that those who laze around in hammocks instead of exercising are more likely to live longer. So when you're lying on the beach, but feel you should be up and about, relax and top up your life account for a while.

But wait, there is another side to this German research coin: Siegfried Lehrl, from the University of Erlangen-Nuremberg, has declared that sunbathing and relaxation actually lowers your IQ. He has even quantified it: apparently two weeks of rest can dent the IQ by 20 points. But active travellers don't have to worry: it's boredom that's the intelligence killer. So, are you Beatles or Stones? Axt or Lehrl?

WHO WEARS SHORT SHORTS?

Would not being able to wear a bikini influence your decision to cancel a trip? Apparently so, if Malaysia is your destination. Much to the dismay of its tourism minister Abdul Kadir Sheikh Fadzir and the tourism sector, the ban on bikinis has resulted in a severe drop in visitor numbers. But it's not just bikinis that are banned, the Muslim Opposition Party, ruling the state of Terengganu, has also segregated men and women at pools and hotels, and has prohibited unisex hair salons, karaoke outlets and pubs. The controversial question is: do tourists have the right to act as they please, even if they are shocking their host country's belief system and culture, or does a state have the right to impose restrictions on people's freedom?

CHEAP HIT

It seems there is a new drug around. It's not class 'A', it's not even class 'B'. In fact, it's what's known as 'getting from A to B'. Too much of anything can be detrimental they say (damn them) and with the advent of low-cost airlines and cheap flights, it seems there is a wave of addicts who just can't get enough of the amazing deals on offer.

A recent survey found that 46% of 18 to 35 year olds have skipped work to take advantage of a cut-price break, 20% have also admitted to missing a family wedding, 36% have missed a date and 37% have missed a friend's birthday. Symptoms of this 'jet pack' are square eyes and twitchy fingers, the result of hours spent mouse-clicking through the internet for the best deals. You will find many of these poor souls in London, where a fifth of this age group survive on at least three such holidays a year. So, if you are accosted in the street, don't be surprised if the question asked is: 'Hey man, got any tickets?'

THE WHO'S WHO OF THE QE2

• The cruise liner Queen Elizabeth 2 moves six inches for each gallon of diesel she burns.

• The ship should always be written QE2 rather than QEII, which is the actual queen (if you bragged about a ride to America on the QEII you might eventually find yourself in prison).

• If preparing a speech about such a voyage, never write about chatting to QEII in a queue about 'who's who' on the QE2, for you are steering yourself into choppy waters.

Blackbeard may have been a pirate, but he insisted that gentlemen should be able to walk the plank with dignity.

TRAVEL TEASERS

Fill in the blanks twice to make two different explorers.
M***O P***
Answer on page 153

LARGEST COUNTRIES NAMED AFTER PEOPLE

1. United States of America
Named after: Amerigo Vespucci
(Italy; 1451–1512)
3,539,245 square miles

2. Saudi Arabia
Named after:
Abdul Aziz ibn-Saud
(Nejd; 1882–1953)
830,000 square miles

3. Bolivia
Named after: Simon Bolivar
(Venezuela; 1783–1830)
418,685 square miles

4. Colombia
Named after:
Christopher Columbus
(Italy; 1451–1506)
401,044 square miles

5. Philippines
Named after: Philipp II
(Spain; 1527–1506)
115,124 square miles

6. Falkland Islands
Named after: Lucius Cary

2nd Viscount Falkland
(UK; 1610–1643)
4,700 square miles

7. Northern Mariana
Named after: Maria Teresa
(Austria; 1717–1780)
184 square miles

8. Wallis and Futuna
Named after: Samuel Wallis
(UK; 1728–1795)
105 square miles

9. Cook Islands
Named after: Captain James
Cook (UK; 1728–1779)
93 square miles

10. Marshall Islands
Named after:
Captain John Marshall
(UK; 1748–c.1818)
70 square miles

*It is debated whether China
was named after the Emperor
Chin… If so, it would
obviously rank first.*

SPACE TRAVEL

The world's leading and lagging airlines:

	First Class	Business	Premium	Economy
Aeroflot	55	38		32
Air Zimbabwe	43			30
Qantas	78	50		31
Cathay Pacific	79	60		32
British Airways	78	73	38	31

*The number is the distance, in inches, between the back of one row
of seats and the back of the row of seats in front.*

Percentage of people who make travel insurance claims 31

FREE AS A BIRD

You're on a jumbo jet, you've taken off and seem to be cruising at a reasonable altitude. Then the captain announces: 'Ladies and gentlemen, it's now safe to undo your seatbelts, your shoes, your trousers, shirts, skirts...'

Yes, the good old US of A have organised the world's first flight for passengers wanting to fly *au naturel* (though they should really use hang-gliders for a more realistic experience).

The flight, from Miami to Mexico, required passengers to be clothed for check-in and take off, but once they were thousands of feet above the rest of us, it was considered safe for them to disrobe. That's one flight on which you definitely wouldn't want to be sitting next to the big fat person.

There was only one extra rule: sex was definitely not permitted during the flight. No, that would be taking it all just too far.

A NO FRILLS COCK-UP

People tend to return from travelling with horror stories of delays, lost passports and hotel mix-ups, but just occasionally, it does work the other way. The Dryer family from Liverpool spotted flights to Florida for £15 each – that's £485 cheaper than they should have been. The family of six enjoyed their trip to Disney World for the grand total of £90, making an even grander saving of £2,910. The travel company blamed one of its website staff, although there were sightings of a large clothed mouse in the company buildings at that time.

ESCAPE TO PYRRHIC VICTORY

We've all heard the epic escape stories of determined and desperate people crossing whole countries, even continents, in order to return home safely. But there are others, which in contrast, seem rather pathetic. Ronald Thomas was serving a 12-year burglary sentence at a state prison in Oklahoma when he managed to escape, steal a prison van, and make his getaway. He drove 150 miles north to Kansas before phoning the police to say that he was lost, and could he go back to jail please. Oh dear. He'd be no good at Monopoly.

QUOTE UNQUOTE

A good traveller is one who does not know where he is going to, and a perfect traveller does not know where he came from.
LIN YUTANG, spiritualist

Montana Testicle Festival
Clinton, Montana, USA
September
Includes live music, the 'Testy Festy Awards', bullshit bingo, body painting, a wet teeshirt competition, a hairy chest contest, loads to drink and of course – tasting some testes. The health conscious needn't worry though: 'they're 70% or more protein and boneless. Oh, and they belong to bulls too.'

World Championship Cardboard Boat Race
Heber Springs, Arkansas, USA
July
Leave it to Bill Clinton's home state to perfect the art of keeping a cardboard boat from sinking. The homemade boats are fashioned from cardboard, duct tape, glue and paint before the race on Greers Ferry Lake.

US International Jousting Competition
Estes Park, Colorado, USA
September
International Jousting Competition held at the Longs Peak Scottish/Irish Highland Festival in Estes Park, Colorado. Some 50,000 people show up to witness not only jousting, but ring spearing, spear throwing and shield hitting.

Deniliquin Play on the Plains and World Record Ute Muster
Deniliquin, NSW, Australia
September/October
A world record bid is held each year on the plains to muster the largest parade of legally-registered utes in the world.

Broomstick Beating Festival,
Mamala and Morella, Indonesia
January
A week after the end of Ramadan the men of these two villages find the time and inclination to beat each other's bare backs with broomsticks. Once the sticks are down, they apply 'mamala oil' made from coconuts to their wounds, apparently giving them supernatural powers. Changing clothes in a phone booth seems tame in comparison. Accept no substitute.

CAN'T PULL, WON'T PAY

One Norwegian man's fruitless romantic pursuits during his holiday have inspired him to claim back its cost. He has applied to his insurance company for compensation for the 'coldness of the pool', the £80 that was stolen from him and the general lack of sexual shenanigans. The very understanding Europeiske Reiseforsikring insurance company, used to bizarre demands, offered to help with the theft but declared: 'the ladies, he'll have to manage all by himself.'

DON'T LEAVE ME HIGH

The highest airport in the world is Bangda in Tibet, at 4,300m (14,100ft). That makes it a little less reassuring to hear the pilot say: 'We are now cruising at 15,000ft'. You'll be pleased to hear, it also has one of the longest runways at 5,500m (18,000ft), presumably to give planes time to take off in the thin Himalayan air.

The two lowest airports in the world both have a rather morbid ring to them. First, there's Furnace Creek Airport in Death Valley National Park, which sits 64m (210ft) below sea level. And, if you really want to limbo in to land, there's Israel's I Bar Yehuda airport near the Dead Sea, which hides away at a shy 386m (1,266ft) below sea level.

And if you're thinking, you'll never visit airports like these, Amsterdam's Schiphol International Airport is a little deeper than 6ft under – it stands at 3m (11ft) below sea level.

TRAVEL TEASERS

Two twins are born 20 minutes apart on a boat. The following year, the younger twin celebrates her birthday. Two days later, her older twin brother celebrates his. How is this possible?

Answer on page 153

BUSIEST INTERNATIONAL AIRPORTS

	Passengers (in 2002)
1. Atlanta, *USA*	76,876,128
2. Chicago, *USA*	66,565,952
3. London Heathrow, *UK*	63,338,641
4. Tokyo, *Japan*	61,079,478
5. Los Angeles, *USA*	56,223,843
6. Dallas/Fort Worth, *USA*	52,828,573
7. Frankfurt/Main, *Germany*	48,450,357
8. Charles de Gaulle, Paris, *France*	48,350,172
9. Amsterdam, *Netherlands*	40,736,009
10. Denver, *USA*	35,651,098

QUOTE UNQUOTE

For my part, I travel not to go anywhere, but to go. I travel for travel's sake. The great affair is to move.
ROBERT LOUIS STEVENSON, writer

TRAVELLING IN DISGUISE

René-Auguste Caillié (1799–1838) was the first European to visit Timbuktu and return. The son of poor French peasants, he was obsessed with the idea of seeing the city, renowned as the African El Dorado. Timbuktu was founded by nomads in the 12th century and it rapidly became a major trading depot for the caravans of the Sahara Desert, as well as a rich Islamic cultural centre. It gained almost mythical status as a city of gold where Europeans were not welcome. Caillié studied Arabic and the Islamic religion during his 11 years of preparation. In April 1827, he left the coast of West Africa for his expedition. He reached the mythical Timbuktu a year later, despite being ill for five of those months. In order to enter the desert city, he disguised himself as an Arab trader as part of a caravan, much to the chagrin of proper European explorers of the era. Unimpressed with Timbuktu which had 'become simply a salt trading outpost filled with mud-walled homes in the middle of a barren desert', he left after two weeks. He returned to Morocco and then home to France. Caillié published three volumes about his travels and was awarded a 10,000-Franc prize from the Geographical Society of Paris.

TRAVEL NOTES

From Valparaiso, Chileans stream in. They bring a pair of boots and a knife, a lamp and a shovel.

The entry to San Francisco Bay is now known as 'the golden gate'. Until yesterday, San Francisco was the Mexican town of Yerbas Buenas. In these lands, usurped from Mexico in the war of conquest, there are three-kilo nuggets of pure gold.

The bay has no room for so many ships. An anchor touches bottom, and adventurers scatter across the mountains. No one wastes time on hellos. The cardsharp buries his patent leather boots in the mud:

'Long live my loaded dice! Long live my jack!'...

...Under her lace sunshade, a good-looking Chilean woman smiles as best she can, squeezed by her corset and by the multitude that sweeps her over the sea of mud paved with broken bottles. In this port she is Rosarito Amestica. She was born Rosarito Izquierdo more years ago than she'll tell, became Rosarito Villaseca in Talcahuano, Rosarita Toro in Talca, and Rosarito Montalva in Valparaiso.

From the stern of a ship, the auctioneer offers ladies to the crowd. He exhibits them and sings their praises, one by one, look gentlemen what a waist what youth what beauty what...

'Who'll give more?' says the auctioneer. 'Who'll give more for this incomparable flower?'

Eduardo Galeano, *The Gold of California*

WHAT TYPE OF TRAVELLER ARE YOU?

In 2002, the Travel Industry Association of America prepared a report on the inclinations of western tourists and their attitudes towards environmental issues. They came up with the definition of 'geotourism', which can be described as: 'tourism that sustains or enhances the geographical character of the place being visited – its environment, culture, aesthetics, heritage and the well-being of its residents'.

The following types of traveller were determined from the survey. Which one are you?

Geo-Savys
- 43 years average age
- 41% have kids in household
- 74% work full/part-time
- 12% are retired
- 44% travelled internationally in past three years

Geo-Savys are more likely than any other group to do the following:
- 83% visit destinations with authentic historic and archaeological sites
- 81% prefer small-scale accommodations run by local people
- 81% travel to experience people, lifestyles and cultures very different from their own
- 80% visit small towns and rural areas
- 73% feel it is important to learn about their destination's people, history, and culture

Urban Sophisticates
- 45 years average age
- 30% have kids in household
- 73% work full/part-time
- 12% are retired
- 73% are past-year air travellers
- 73% of Urban Sophisticates prefer trips to destinations offering authentic historic or archaeological sites
- 86% take trips where they can spend time exploring historic and charming towns and locations
- 74% of Urban Sophisticates prefer destinations that offer a wide variety of cultural/arts events and attractions
- 63% of Urban Sophisticates also enjoy visiting large cities, as well as high quality accommodations with excellent facilities and fine dining

Good Citizens
- 55 years average age
- 28% have kids in household
- 54% work full/part-time
- 34% are retired
- 38% travelled internationally in past three years

When they travel, Good Citizens are more likely than others to want to have the following:
- 88% want high levels of cleanliness
- 79% want high levels of safety and security
- 60% want high quality visitor services and personnel

- 43% want to meet travellers who share their interests

Traditionals
- 58 years average age
- 24% have kids in household
- 43% work full/part-time
- 42% are retired

Traditionals are conservative travellers and more likely than any other group to do the following:
- 65% seek no surprises when they travel
- 77% prefer family-friendly destinations
- 66% prefer trips to places where their families were from
- 53% prefer groups tours with pre-set itineraries and tour guides
- 45% like to meet other travellers who share their interests

Wishful Thinkers
- 32 years average age
- 50% have kids in household
- 81% work full/part-time
- 3% are retired
- 24% travelled internationally in past three years

Wishful Thinkers are most interested in outdoor-related travel and show above-average interest in the following:
- 48% like outdoor adventure travel that involves challenge, risk and excitement
- 46% like to travel to remote locales
- 42% like trips to go hunting and fishing
- 35% like primitive travel in the wilderness

They are also above-average in their interest in trips to large cities (54%), high quality accommodations with excellent facilities and fine dining (54%), and luxury and pampering (45%).

Apathetics
- 46 years average age
- 42% have kids in household
- 67% work full/part-time
- 17% are retired
- 18% travelled internationally in past three years

Apathetics, when they travel, seek the following:
- 89% want high levels of cleanliness
- 835 want high levels of safety and security
- 65% want no surprises
- 62% want many forms of entertainment at their destinations, such as nightlife, fine dining, shows and casinos
- 51% say they don't eat unfamiliar foods when travelling

A BRIEF LAMA DRAMA

The one-l lama, he's a priest.
The two-l llama, he's a beast.
And I will bet a silk pajama
There isn't any three-l llama.

Ogden Nash, *The Lama*

DISTINCTIVE DWELLINGS

Underwater hideaway, Florida, USA

For a splashing good time, spend a night at Jules' Undersea Lodge, allegedly the first and only underwater hotel. The watery retreat was previously a research laboratory but opened in 1986 as a luxury retreat for divers. The only way to reach the hotel is by scuba diving being as it is, five fathoms under the surface of a mangrove lagoon. But don't worry if you're not up on your scuba, a three-hour class will qualify inexperienced guests to make the trip.

After arriving in the underwater world, guest can enjoy unlimited dive trips and a gourmet dinner and breakfast prepared by the lodge's very own mer-chef. Might fish be on the menu, per chance?

AKA

Nicknames for some American cities

Boston, MA	*Beantown*
San Francisco, CA	*Golden Gate City*
Savannah, GA	*Garden City*
New Orleans, LA	*Crescent City*
Los Angeles, CA	*City of Angels*
Philadelphia, PA	*City of Brotherly Love*
New York City, NY	*Big Apple*
Dayton, OH	*Birthplace of Aviation*
Chicago, IL	*Second City*
International Fall, MN	*Icebox of the US*
Denver, CO	*Mile-high City*
Pittsburgh, PA	*Iron City*
Detroit, MI	*Motown*
Nashville, TN	*Music City*
Akron, OH	*Rubber City*
Hollywood, CA	*Tinseltown*
Portland, OR	*Rose City*
Indianapolis, IN	*Monument City*

QUOTE UNQUOTE

Beneath this slab
John Brown is stowed.
He watched the ads,
And not the road.
OGDEN NASH, US humorist

Travel, in the younger sort, is a part of education; in the elder, a part of experience. He that travelleth into a country, before he hath some entrance into the language, goeth to school, and not to travel. That young men travel under some tutor or grave servant, I allow well; so that he be such a one that hath the language, and hath been in the country before; whereby he may be able to tell them what things are worthy to be seen in the country where they go, what acquaintances they are to seek, what exercises or discipline the place yieldeth; for else young men shall go hooded, and look abroad little. It is a strange thing, that in sea voyages, where there is nothing to be seen but sky and sea, men should make diaries; but in land travel, wherein so much is to be observed, for the most part they omit it; as if chance were fitter to be registered than observation: let diaries, therefore, be brought in use...If you will have a young man to put his travel into a little room, and in short time to gather much, this you must do: first, as was said, he must have some entrance into the language before he goeth; then he must have such a servant or tutor, as knoweth the country, as was likewise said: let him carry with him also some card, or book, describing the country where he travelleth, which will be a good key to his inquiry; let him keep also a diary; let him not stay long in one city or town, more or less as the place deserveth, but not long; nay, when he stayeth in one city or town, let him change his lodging from one end and part of the town to another, which is a great adamant of acquaintance; let him sequester himself from the company of his countrymen, and diet in such places where there is good company of the nation where he travelleth: let him, upon his removes from one place to another, procure recommendation to some person of quality residing in the place whither he removeth, that he may use his favour in those things he desireth to see or know; thus he may abridge his travel with much profit... When a traveller returneth home, let him not leave the countries where he hath travelled altogether behind him, but maintain a correspondence by letters with those of his acquaintance which are of most worth; and let his travel appear rather in his discourse than in his apparel or gesture; and in his discourse let him be rather advised in his answers, than forward to tell stories: and let it appear that he doth not change his country manners for those of foreign parts; but only prick in some flowers of that he hath learned abroad into the customs of his own country.

Francis Bacon, *Of Travel*

Number of people out of 160 sufferers of deep vein thrombosis who had been 39 *on journeys of four hours or more in the previous month*

THE SIGNS AREN'T GOOD

Outside a Paris dress shop:
Dresses for street walking.

In a Czechoslovakian tourist agency:
Take one of our horse-driven city tours – we guarantee no miscarriages.

In a Rhodes tailor shop:
Order your summers suit. Because is big rush we will execute customers in strict rotation.

A sign posted in Germany's Black Forest:
It is strictly forbidden on our Black Forest camping site that people of different sex, for instance, men and women, live together in one tent unless they are married with each other for that purpose.

In a Zurich hotel:
Because of the impropriety of entertaining guests of the opposite sex in the bedroom, it is suggested that the lobby be used for this purpose.

In an advertisement by a Hong Kong dentist:
Teeth extracted by the latest Methodists.

In a Rome laundry:
Ladies, leave your clothes here and spend the afternoon having a good time.

MOST EXPENSIVE COUNTRIES IN WHICH TO BUY A BIG MAC

1. Iceland	US$5.51
2. Switzerland	US$4.56
3. Sweden	US$3.46
4. UK	US$3.19
5. Malta	US$3.03
6. Euro Area	US$2.87
7. South Korea	US$2.73
8. USA	US$2.65
9. United Arab Emirates	US$2.45
10. Saudi Arabia	US$2.40

A MAN FOR ALL REASONS

St Christopher is not only the patron saint of travellers, he can also be called upon by:
Car drivers • Taxi drivers • Bachelors
Baden • Germany • Boatmen • Bookbinders • Brunswick
Bus drivers • Fruit dealers • Gardeners • St Kitts

The good fellow can also be relied upon for protection against lightning, pestilential archers, floods, hailstorms and toothache.

Amount, in dollars, that American Airlines saved in 1987 by eliminating one olive from each salad served in first class

'Ah, no, Mr President,' said the helpful aide, 'the pretty boat goes over here, in the big water.'

SURVIVAL TIPS

Water

In a disaster situation a good cup of tea restores morale. Tea quenches thirst; coffee exacerbates it.

Finding water in a survival situation must be the first priority.

Be suspicious of any pool with no green vegetation growing around it or with bones lying around the side.

Always boil water collected from wild pools or rivers.

The average person loses about five pints of water a day. Fluid loss can be reduced by: avoiding exertion; not smoking, staying in the shade; eating as little as possible as digestion draws water from the vital organs into the digestive tract; never drinking alcohol when water is scarce; trying not to talk; keeping clothes on to prevent excess water loss by sweat drying on the skin.

After a long period of dehydration, a person will vomit if they gulp water too fast, so take small sips at first.

Never drink urine or sea water because of the high salt content which will cause further dehydration.

If desperate, animal eyes, including salt water fish, are a good source of pure water.

TRAVEL TEASERS

Unscramble the following to make a country:
LAFND
Answer on page 153

FLYING LANDMARKS

17 December, 1903
Orville and Wilbur Wright's 1903 Wright Flyer made the first successful flight by a powered, heavier-than-air machine. Orville Wright piloted the first flight – which lasted 12 seconds and covered 120ft.

21 May, 1927
Charles A Lindbergh completed the first solo non-stop transatlantic flight in history. The Spirit of St Louis made the 3,610-mile flight from Long Island, New York, to Paris, France, in 33 hours, 30 minutes.

14 October, 1947
A Bell X-1 – named 'Glamorous Glennis' by its pilot, US Air Force Captain Charles E 'Chuck' Yeager – became the first plane to fly faster than the speed of sound. The X-1 reached a speed of 700 miles per hour at an altitude of 43,000ft.

10 January, 1980
David J Springbett completed the fastest around the world flight using scheduled aircraft in 44 hours, six minutes.

23 April, 1984
Kanellos Kanellopoulos made the longest-ever flight in a human-powered aircraft, travelling 71 miles.

20 November, 1984
Pilot Julian RP Nott and crewman Spider Anderson set a world altitude record for a pressurised balloon, flying 17,766ft.

16 August, 1995
The Concorde completed the fastest around-the-world flight by a commercial jet in 31 hours, 27 minutes and 49 seconds.

1 March, 1999
The first successful non-stop flight around the world in a balloon. Bertrand Piccard and Brian Jones made the 28,431-mile journey from Château d'Oex in the Swiss Alps to the Egyptian desert in 19 days, 21 hours, and 55 minutes.

QUOTE UNQUOTE

Maybe this world is another planet's Hell.
ALDOUS HUXLEY, writer

OLD POSTER, NEW CAPTION

'No, you fool', groaned Stephenson. 'Not that type of rocket!'

BRITISH CONSULATES CAN...

...issue emergency passports
...contact relatives to ask them to help a traveller in distress
...cash a cheque, in an emergency, of up to £100 (as long as it's
backed by a valid bank card)
...help find local lawyers, interpreters and doctors
...arrange for a next of kin to be informed about death
and advise on procedures
...visit you if you're arrested or in prison and arrange for messages to
be sent to relatives or friends
...put you in touch with organisations who help trace missing persons
...speak to local authorities on your behalf

Only as a last resort will they lend you money to get you home.

AHOY THERE

There's low self esteem, and then there's low self a'steam... Inspired by
Dorian Gray's words ('Live the wonderful life that is in you. Be afraid
of nothing'), US adventurer Richard Halliburton paid the lowest ever
toll to cross the Panama Canal when he swam it in 1928. The
authorities had told him that the locks would only be filled for a ship,
so he declared himself the SS Halliburton and was granted passage
through. Like all other vessels, his toll was assessed by his tonnage; he
weighed 140lb, and so paid 36 cents. It's a wonder there are not more
HMS Backpackers to be found these days.

GIVE THE WORLD A BREAK

Shop and eat locally
By avoiding all-inclusive tour packages that seep up to 80% of tourist profits, your spendings can directly benefit the local places and people you visit.

Do your research in advance
Knowing the customs and the politico-social frame of the country in addition to the places to visit beforehand will deepen a visitor's appreciation of and interaction with the locals and their environment.

Make use of public transport
Rather than renting a car, public transport is the best way to diminish your environmental footprint and meet people.

The grass is not always greener on the other side
Concentrate on the beautiful assets your nearby area has to offer to reduce long-distance travel.

Give respectfully
Offering useful gifts such as school materials, donations or staple foods through established structures of authority, usually a village chief or head of family, is the most effective way to show your appreciation.

QUOTE UNQUOTE

A continent ages quickly once we come to it.
ERNEST HEMINGWAY, writer and adventurer

SIGNS YOU FLY TOO MUCH

- You have a favourite trolley at the airport.
- You can mime along with the safety announcement.
- As far as you're concerned, more than five peanuts at a time is just plain indulgent.
- Jet lag is your normal state.
- You think drinks only come in single serving sized bottles and are mystified about the 'oversized' bottles at the supermarket.
- You are surprised at the cinema when you don't have to use headphones or crane your neck 45 degrees to see the screen.
- You are continually amazed when there is no queue for the bathroom when you are at home.
- You find metal cutlery too heavy and slightly unnerving when it doesn't take 20 minutes to saw through a piece of meat.
- You know the duty-free catalogue off by heart.
- You have enough mini tubes of toothpaste to last you for the rest of your life.

For carrying my clothes, books, etc, 8 boxes of different sizes, watertight, well rounded at the edges, not more than 10 inches deep, and not very wide, so that they may be easily grasped when on the shoulder or head. The larger boxes are for carrying clothes only, the smaller for a mixture of clothes with heavier articles, such as books, boots, etc. None of the boxes when filled to weigh over 50lbs.

For clothing I have provided 1 ordinary suit of tweed clothes for the colder regions, 3 suits of tropical tweeds, and as many thin jerseys; 6 pairs of thick woollen stockings or socks; 1 pair of strong boots, for wet season; 2 pairs of lighter make, for the dry season, and 2 pairs of canvas shoes for camp use, and when feet are sore. Heavy boots are to be condemned for the tropics, as the feet soon become scalding hot, making travelling in the heat of the day most painful.

I have formed a very decided opinion as to the necessity of the African traveller making himself as comfortable in camp as the circumstances and the extent of the expedition will permit. The climate is so trying and varied, that to attempt 'to rough it' unnecessarily is simply to invite disease, and too often death.

Impressed by experience with these convictions, I have been careful to select a fairly roomy tent, 9 feet long, of good canvas. An iron bedstead, with a cork bed, and two warm Austrian blankets. A folding chair, camp-stool, and a small portable table. The latter is an immense convenience when much writing has to be done...

Among other useful articles the following may be mentioned: Waterproof ground sheets; roll-up case of tools; one .577 Express rifle, one .577 reduced to .450, a 12 bore gun, a revolver, with ammunition to suit; two axes; a hunting knife; two bill-hooks and two reaping-hooks, to be used in camping and cutting a way through jungle and forest; diary and necessary stationery; some books, especially such as can be read and re-read.'

Mr Thomson's journey across Masai land in 1883, taken from the Royal Geographical Society's *Hints to Travellers* for African travellers.

QUOTE UNQUOTE

They say travel broadens the mind; but you must have the mind.
GK CHESTERTON, writer

STRANGE WEE BEASTIE

Love it or hate it, trophy hunting was often a part of travelling for gentlemen in the past, bringing a sense of adventure, danger to their trips and prestige upon themselves. Hunting tigers in India, big game hunting in Africa, perhaps an epic struggle with a marlin out in the open ocean... and what about a Hemingwayesque battle with a fierce, wild haggis in Scotland? A third of American tourists believe a haggis is a real animal, and almost a quarter arrive in Scotland hoping to hunt one down. A haggis on the wall next to the stag's head would complete an impressive collection.

BECKS AND BEATRIX

Fascinating culture, stunning scenery, delicious cuisine: there are many reasons why we choose the holiday destinations we choose. So you might expect the same from those visiting our shores. Perhaps visitors want to see for themselves the architecture of Buckingham Palace and Westminster Abbey, or perhaps they want to take in the rolling English hills or taste fish and chips while sitting on an English seaside. But then again, maybe not. It seems the Japanese come for some completely different reasons.

Following the popularity of the England captain in Japan during the 2002 World Cup, the Japan Travel Bureau is planning 'Beckham tours' to his birthplace in East London, his school in East Chingford and Old Trafford. Presumably followed by a hop across to Madrid. That's 14 hours and 6,000 odd miles to come and see a footballer's house. Pretty crazy, huh? Then again perhaps not. According to the Japan Travel Bureau, the second most popular attraction for Japanese tourists is none other than an imaginary bunny rabbit, whose creator has been dead for over 60 years. Peter Rabbit more popular than Big Ben? Who'd have thought it?

FANTASTIC FESTIVITIES

St John's Pig Parade, Balayan, Philippines, *June*
To celebrate San Juan Bautista (John the Baptist), every June the people of Balayan put together a parade. But it's not just any parade: dozens of fully clothed roast suckling pigs are carried through the town on litters, sitting up on little chairs, like people. The baptism of St John is re-enacted in the festival, which includes a lot of water. So don't be surprised when a huge water fights break out and unsuspecting passers-by become the target for a good dousing.

Prince Edward Island, Canada
Renamed in honour of Edward,
Duke of Kent (father of Queen
Victoria) in 1799

Tasmania, Australia
Named after Dutch navigator
Abel Tasman who first sighted it
in 1642

The Cook Islands,
New Zealand
Named after English sea captain
James Cook who explored them
in 1773 and 1777

Victoria Falls,
Zimbabwe, Zambia
Explorer David Livingstone
named them after Queen
Victoria in 1855

Athens, Greece
Named after Athena, goddess of
wisdom and knowledge

Wiencke Island, Antarctica
Named after a Norwegian sailor

aboard the 1897–1899 Belgica
scientific expedition to the
South Pole.

Cody, Wyoming,
The Rocky Mountain States,
USA
Named after Buffalo Bill Cody in
1896 when its founder, a real-
estate speculator, wanted to use
it to attract settlers

Bermuda
Named after the sea captain Juan
de Bermudez, who first sited the
islands somewhere around 1503

Williamsburg,
Virginia, USA
Named after King William of
Orange during his reign

Jaipur, India
Named after the warrior and
astronomer Maharaja Jai Singh
II who lived from 1693 to 1743.
He planned and founded the
famous pink city

BOXED

Some people will do anything to get where they want to go
without paying, not least dodging a train or a bus fare by hiding
in the toilet. But to avoid paying a US$320 plane ticket, you need
to take it to the next level.

Twenty-five year old Charles D McKinley, a 5ft 9in shipping clerk
from Brooklyn, New York, climbed inside a shipping crate 3ft
wide and 3ft deep (and you thought economy class was cramped)
and airmailed himself to Texas to see his folks. He would have
gotten away with it had he not popped up on arrival to shake the
delivery driver's hand. He was reported and charged as a
stowaway, a federal misdemeanour.

TRAVELLING BOOKS

In 2003, the BBC ran a poll to discover the nation's favourite novels. Several of the titles that made the final cut sound like travelling classics. The books, in their final positions, were:

4. *The Hitchhiker's Guide to the Galaxy*, Douglas Adams
48. *Far from the Madding Crowd*, Thomas Hardy
63. *A Tale of Two Cities*, Charles Dickens
87. *Brave New World*, Aldous Huxley
90. *On The Road*, Jack Kerouac
101. *Three Men in a Boat*, Jerome K Jerome
146. *The Green Mile*, Stephen King
164. *The Shipping News*, Annie Proulx
173. *The Old Man and the Sea*, Ernest Hemingway

DISTINCTIVE DWELLINGS

Salt Palace and Spa Hotel, Salar de Uyuni, Bolivia.
The weary traveller, wandering on the prehistoric and surreal salt flats 12,500ft up in the south-west of Bolivia, will no doubt think he has been there slightly too long when he sees this hotel made almost entirely out of sodium carbonate (for want of a livelier euphemism). The roof, walls, bar, tables and chairs, even the beds (will this please the weary traveller?) are all made of salt.

The hotel was built in 1993 by one Juan Quesada, who saw the salt, saw the tourists that flocked to this magical site (it's one of Bolivia's main attractions), and brought them together in this 'first' for the hotel and catering industry. Twelve guest rooms with 24 beds and shared bathrooms surround a central courtyard. Rather like ice, salt makes for good building blocks. The sun heats it in the day and at night, when temperatures drop below freezing outside, the guests remain snug within.

Apparently there's a notice asking customers not to lick the walls so the place doesn't disappear. It would certainly be a good place for tequila parties.

NEW WORLDS

Travelling has always represented new horizons, not least for the millions of people who emigrated to America with the hope of a starting a better life for themselves and their families. Charlie Chaplin was discovered by producer Mack Sennett while he was travelling with a British troupe touring America in 1913. Sennett signed him for US$150 a week, and within just seven years he had appeared in 69 films and was earning US$10,000 a week.

48 *Age, in hours, before which a baby should not fly because its heart and lungs are unable to cope with reduced levels of oxygen*

WORLD FIRSTS

1st motorway: the German autobahn opened May 1921

1st UK motorway: the M1, opened in 1959. The first section was 72 miles long and cost £50 million to build

1st UK train buffet car: on the LMS train service from Euston to Nottingham in 1932

1st fare-paying passenger flight in the UK: from Brooklands to Hendon in 1911

1st motorised coach tour: the six-day continental excursion from Paris to Aix-les-bains in 1898

1st duty-free shop: opened in Shannon airport in 1947; at first, it stocked neither tobacco nor alcohol

BEACH BOMBS

When we travel to countries with warmer climes we may realistically worry about certain things. We might be afraid of snakes, or scorpions. We might be afraid to go in the water, fearful of what is lurking in the depths.

But we should actually be more afraid of sitting in the shade: falling coconuts kill around 150 people every year, 10 times more than those killed by sharks.

British travel insurance company Club Direct now provides insurance against these lethal beach bombs, which, on their short journey south from the branch, reach speeds of 50 miles an hour and can land on a person with a force greater than one tonne. Ow.

The subject was looked into in detail by one Professor Peter Barss, of McGill University in Montreal, who won the 2001 IG Nobel Prize for Medicine (Awarding Institution: the Annals of Improbable Research) for his paper 'Injuries due to falling coconuts'.

BIBLE TOPS NEW CHART

What does God have to do with shower caps, sweets on the pillow and trouser presses? Apparently he's less useful than all of them.

Travelling business executives consider the good book, distributed free by the Gideon Society, as the most useless item available to them in a hotel room, pipping pillows and presses to the post. It's not much of a surprise to find they preferred internet connections and phone chargers, but when it was revealed that only 2% said they wanted adult TV channels, the credibility of the whole survey was called into question. An almighty reprieve.

SURVIVAL TIPS

Cold

Avoid walking on icebergs as they can turn over without warning.

Should you ever kill a polar bear or seal, don't eat their livers as they contain toxic quantities of vitamin A.

Avoid falling into ice-cold water. Exposed parts will freeze in about four minutes, you will be unconsciousness in seven minutes and death will occur in 15 minutes.

In cold climates, cold wind can freeze unprotected flesh in minutes.

Wool is best for inner garments: cotton absorbs moisture and if you're wearing wet cotton, you can lose heat 240 times faster than when the cotton is dry. If necessary remove cotton clothes and dry them individually.

To avoid frostbite, contract and relax your face to stop stiff patches forming and to exercise muscles. Keep hands moving too or your fingers will freeze and fall off. The first signs of frostbite are waxy, blackened or reddening skin. Ears, nose and fingers are most at risk.

Tight clothing reduces circulation and quickens frostbite.

Get rid of any snow on the body before taking shelter; it will turn to water, dampen clothing and reduce temperature.

Keep gloves on and keep them dry.

Spilt petrol will freeze flesh instantly and cause frostbite far quicker than water.

Tiredness increases the risk of frostbite so rest is important.

Avoid camping in hollows as this is where frost collects.

HANDY HOWDIES

Japanese	*Konnichi wa*
Macedonian	*Zdravo*
Nepali	*Namaste*
Norwegian	*Nei*
Portuguese	*Ola*
Russian	*Privet*
Swahili	*Jambo*
Thai	*Sawat dii*
Welsh	*Dydd da*

QUOTE UNQUOTE

Americans are rather like bad Bulgarian wine: they don't travel well.
BERNARD FALK, journalist

LEFT OR RIGHT?

In 1998, a Roman quarry was discovered at Blunsdon Ridge near Swindon with an access road leading to the rock face. There were two sets of cart tracks: the one on the left, facing the quarry wall, was shallow, while the departing tracks, on the right, were deep from the weight. We can therefore conclude that the Romans drove on the left-hand side in Britain.

Roman coins have also been found depicting horse riders passing one another right shoulder to right shoulder. This is further proof of keeping to the left in ancient times.

TRAVEL TEASERS

There was an airplane crash in which every single person died. There were two survivors. How is this possible?
Answer on page 153

WHY DO THE BRAZILIANS SPEAK PORTUGUESE?

Four years before Christopher Columbus landed on what he thought was Japan, Bartolomeu Dias reached the southernmost tip of Africa. The powerful rulers of Spain and Portugal thus turned to the Pope to help set up Christian rule in the new-found territories. In 1455, Pope Calixtus III divided the world between Spain and Portugal, giving one the north and the other the south of the Canary Islands. But this didn't seem fair.

With the untold riches that potentially existed below the equator and the New World of the Americas holding much promise, Pope Alexander VI Borgia redivided the world between Spain and Portugal according to a meridian stretching from Pole to Pole 100 leagues to the west of Cape Verde. On 7 June 1494, the Treaty of Tordesillas moved the boundary 270 leagues west. And this is why Portuguese is spoken in Brazil, and Spanish is spoken throughout the rest of South America.

I opened the bag and packed the boots in; and then, just as I was going to close it, a horrible idea occurred to me. Had I packed my tooth-brush? I don't know how it is, but I never do know whether I've packed my tooth-brush.

My tooth-brush is a thing that haunts me when I'm travelling, and makes my life a misery. I dream that I haven't packed it, and wake up in a cold perspiration, and get out of bed and hunt for it. And, in the morning, I pack it before I have used it, and have to unpack again to get it, and it is always the last thing I turn out of the bag; and then I repack and forget it, and have to rush upstairs for it at the last moment and carry it to the railway station, wrapped up in my pocket-handkerchief.

Of course I had to turn every mortal thing out now, and, of course, I could not find it. I rummaged the things up into much the same state that they must have been before the world was created, and when chaos reigned. Of course, I found George's and Harris's eighteen times over, but I couldn't find my own. I put the things back one by one, and held everything up and shook it. Then I found it inside a boot. I repacked once more.

When I had finished, George asked if the soap was in. I said I didn't care a hang whether the soap was in or whether it wasn't; and I slammed the bag to and strapped it, and found that I had packed my tobacco-pouch in it, and had to re-open it. It got shut up finally at 10.50 p.m.

Jerome K Jerome, *Three Men in a Boat*

JOURNEY'S END

Pamela Digby Churchill Hayward Harriman

Pamela Digby Churchill Hayward Harriman, Bill Clinton's Madame Ambassador to Paris, died doing laps in the pool at the Ritz where she used to meet her personal trainer every morning. This girl was quite a traveller: in the spirit of her great great great something aunt, Jane Digby, she'd started off travelling from Dorset to London, where she married Winston Churchill's son Randolph. She moved on from him to Paris (where she famously had an affair with Eli de Rothschild), to Italy (where she was 'great' friends with Gianni Agnelli) and then to America where she worked her way through men and states, ending up with Averill Harriman whom she'd first been involved with in London during World War II. After his death, her tireless devotion to the Democrat cause was rewarded with a ticket to the American Embassy in Paris, where she and her art collection were duly installed and where she lived until the day she died.

Zigzagging across the waters of the Pacific Ocean near the 180-degree meridian, the International Date Line (IDL) is plotted on today's charts and globes to indicate the boundary line between 'today' and 'tomorrow'. But despite its name, the precise location of the IDL is not fixed by any international law, treaty or agreement.

Possibly the earliest reference to the date line is found in the works of a Syrian prince and geographer-historian Abu'l-Fida (1273–1331). In his *Taqwin al-Buldan*, Abu'l-Fida described how a traveller, depending on his direction of travel, would either lose or gain a day at the completion of his circumnavigation.

It was Antonio Pigafetta (c.1490–c.1535), the Italian who chronicled the first circumnavigation of the world by the Portuguese explorer and navigator Ferdinand Magellan (c.1480–1521), who first mentioned the peculiar incident of 'losing' a whole day.

A date line was adopted in the Pacific Ocean, but has only ever been defined by cartographers.

In October 1884, representatives from 25 countries convened in Washington at the International Meridian Conference to recommend a common prime meridian for geographical and nautical charts that would be acceptable to all parties concerned.

Due to the lack of any international guidelines for the location of the date line, 20th-century mapmakers have tended to follow the recommendations of the British and the American Navy. The earliest recommendations issued by these departments referring to the date line appear to date from 1899 and 1900.

The most recent major adjustment of the IDL was announced in 1994 by the government of Kiribati. This extended group of islands has formed an independent republic within the British Commonwealth since 1979 and consists of some 33 small atolls. For many years the IDL bisected the island republic into two halves so that the western part of the republic was always 24 hours ahead of its eastern part, and there were only four days in each week when official business could be conducted. To remedy this situation, on 1 January 1995, the IDL was altered to run along the many-cornered eastern boundary of the republic. This line became significant during the Millennium celebrations when Kiribati become a serious contender in the race for the place in the Pacific to best view the first rays of the rising sun at the begin of the new millennium.

The props department had done it again: Yorick was supposed to be a skull, not a scroll.

HELP!

Useful numbers for the Foreign Office

Main switchboard	00 44 20 7008 5100
Services for Britons overseas	00 44 20 7008 0218
Travel Advice	00 44 87 0606 0290
Visa Enquiries	00 44 20 7008 8438

We sent for this guide, who told us he would undertake to carry us the same way with no hazard from the snow, provided we were armed sufficiently to protect our selves from wild beasts; for he said, upon these great snows, it was frequent for some wolves to show themselves at the foot of the mountains, being made ravenous for want of food, the ground being covered with snow. We told him we were well enough prepared for such creatures as they were, if he would ensure us from a kind of two-legged wolves, which we were told we were in most danger from, especially on the French side of the mountains.

He satisfy'd us there was no danger of that kind in the way we were to go; so we readily agreed to follow him, as did also twelve other gentlemen, with their servants, some French, some Spanish; who as I said, had attempted to go, and were obliged to come back again.

Accordingly, we set out from Pampeluna, with out guide on the fifteenth of November; and indeed, I was surprised, when instead of going forward, he came directly back with us on the same road that we came from Madrid, above twenty miles; when being passed two rivers, and come into the plain country, we found our selves in a warm climate again, where the country was pleasant, and no snow to be seen; but on a sudden, turning to his left, he approached the mountains another way; and though it is true, the hills and precipices looked dreadful, yet he made so many tours, such meanders, and led us by such winding ways, that we were insensibly passed the height of the mountains, without being much incumbered with the snow, and all on a sudden he shewed us the pleasant fruitful provinces of Languedoc and Gascoign, all green and flourishing.

Daniel Defoe, *Robinson Crusoe*

FANTASTIC FESTIVITIES

Festa de Sao Joao, Oporto, Portugal, *June*
This festival involves the inhabitants of the town running around and hitting each other over the head with plastic hammers and heads of garlic. The exact reasons for this are no longer known, but the festival is practiced every 23 and 24 June nonetheless. The whole town also turns out on the streets for bonfires, eating and drinking and the party lasts all night.

La Noche de Rabanos, Oaxaca, Mexico, *December*
The humble radish becomes the building block of life in December, as inhabitants create animals, vehicles and landscape scenes from this multi-talented vegetable. Inspiration is fuelled throughout the day by tequila, which possibly helps. It is also customary to chuck your plate over your shoulder after tucking in.

SUFFERING FROM WIND

The Atlantic hurricane season officially blows from 1 June to 30 November. These dates encompass over 97% of tropical gales, which reach their peak in early to mid September.

The North-east Pacific basin receives its hurricane activity from late May or early June to late October or early November. The storms peak in late August or early September.

The North-west Pacific basin suffers from tropical cyclones all year round, although there is a distinct drop in February and the first half of March and an increase from July to November with a peak in late August or early September.

The North Indian basin has a double peak of hurricane activity in May and November, although tropical cyclones are also witnessed from April to December.

The South-west Indian and Australian and South-east Indian basins have very similar annual cycles with tropical cyclones beginning in late October or early November and ending in May.

The South-west Pacific basin begins its tropical cyclone activity in late October or early November. It reaches a single peak in late February or early March, and then fades out in early May.

Globally, September is the most active month for hurricanes with May escaping the most unscathed.

QUOTE UNQUOTE

At my age travel broadens the behind.
STEPHEN FRY, writer and humorist

BIG GIRL

One of New York's most famous monuments, the Statue of Liberty is not actually American. It was constructed in France in 1875 and was presented to the US on its completion on 4 July 1884 in recognition of the Franco-american friendship established during the American Revolution. On her completion, Liberty had to make her own journey over the Atlantic: she was dismantled and shipped to the US in 350 individual pieces in 214 crates, and was then rebuilt in 1886.

When the US opened up its borders to immigration in the 19th and early 20th centuries, it was this statue that the arriving hopefuls first saw before landing on Ellis Island where they were either allowed in or turned away.

INTERESTING FOREIGN SECRETARIES

19–22 December 1783: The 1st Marquess of Buckingham was the shortest serving Foreign Secretary.

1807–1089: George Canning had policy differences with his cabinet colleague Castlereagh (the Secretary of State for War) which led to a duel in which Canning was wounded in the leg. This is the last time cabinet ministers are known for sure to have fought it out.

1834–1835: The first Duke of Wellington's idea of foreign policy was to: 'stand well with France and distrust Russia'.

1886: Lord Rosebery achieved his three most treasured ambitions by the age of 48: he'd become Prime Minister, won the Derby and married an heiress.

1905–1916: Viscount Grey was the longest serving Foreign Secretary. It was from his room that he observed the 'lamps going out all over Europe'.

1935–1938: Sir Anthony Eden broadened the basis of recruitment into the Foreign Office so that you no longer had to be independently wealthy to serve there.

1938–1940: Lord Halifax; he once mistook Hitler for a doorman.

21ST CENTURY NOMADS

The Innu are the traditional followers of the migrating herds of Canadian caribou in eastern Canada's Labrador peninsula. First they hunted them with spears and arrows, then with muskets and now with rifles. And these days, instead of walking to the hunting site or even riding there on a hunting sledge, they take snowmobiles or even fly there by helicopter. In winter, the herds of caribou roam the frozen, windswept plateau of the Barren Grounds. Here, in campsites, the hunters leave their tents at daybreak and share their catches at a communal feast at night. The feast won't necessarily consist just of caribou, but fish, game birds and even fox or roasted porcupine can be added to the menu.

Unfortunately, this is a lifestyle slowly being eroded as expeditions, such as those to hunt the caribou, become ever harder as the ancestral hunting grounds are violated by mining operations and swept by low-flying jets on training exercises.

If you want to visit not just another place, but another time, these locations can help you along:

Sukhotai, Thailand

Sukhotai was originally a Khmer settlement, but was rebuilt around 1290, and was the centre of a wealthy kingdom until 1438. Thailand's first capital still boasts beautiful temple ruins, stupas (shrines) and images of the walking Buddhas.

Mistras, Greece

From the early 1300s, Mistras flourished as a centre for Byzantine Renaissance. The philosopher Plethon lived here in the 1500s. He 'discovered' Plato and was the protege of the last Byzantine Emperor. Well-preserved churches with striking marble iconostases and frescoes, and views of Sparta, once the military capital of the world, contribute to this ruined city's uniqueness.

Santiago de Compostela, Spain.

St James's body was rediscovered here in the 9th century, after 750 years of being lost. Santiago de Compostela became a great pilgrim centre, inspired the world's first travel guide, and attracted more than 500,000 visitors each year during the 11th and 12th centuries. The shrine in the cathedral continues to draw many people, especially via the old walking routes through France and Spain.

Amalfi, Italy

Amalfi was once a renowned maritime trading republic. Two centuries after its beginnings in the 9th century, the Mariner's Compass was invented here and some of the largest ships on the Mediterranean were built and sent off to transport crusaders to the Holy Land. The town's architecture reflects its Arabic and Byzantine influences and a tradition in papermaking.

Machu Picchu, Peru

The city of the Incas was built in the 15th century at the height of the Inca Empire. As it was only rediscovered and exposed to the West in 1911, it escaped the Spanish conquest, and remains an awe-inspiring ruined city, perched 2,500m above sea level on the Andean mountain range.

TRAVEL TEASERS

Where in Africa?
C
GO
Answer on page 153

During the Victorian era, the increasing prosperity of the British upper middle class led to a growth in travel and a corresponding demand for reliable travel information. In 1836, John Murray III of London wrote and published the first modern guidebook, initiating a wide-ranging and comprehensive series that dispensed accurate information and advice for the sophisticated and affluent traveller's journeys 'in season' and winter sojourns in warmer climates.

Carefully researched and written by well-educated Britons (or local experts writing in English) who were often prominent or destined to become so, *Murray's Handbooks* were the most popular guidebooks for British travellers in the 19th century.

In addition to practical information, advice, and itineraries set forth in abundant detail, the guides contained vivid accounts of abandoned ruins, tortuous journeys along primitive roads, and scenic marvels. The volumes also featured summaries of the nation's history, geography, demographics, culture, and climate, along with maps and plans.

Within individual countries there were sometimes separate series for different areas. For instance, there was a series for northern Germany and one for southern Germany. Similarly, there was a separate series on Paris and many series on the counties of Britain.

'These *Murray's Handbooks* for travellers of the last century are wonderful books, full of meticulous and graphic descriptions of a vanished world. In their downright tone you see, too, as clear a picture of the Imperial Englishman on his travels as you see of the lands he travelled through, so that to read them is like overhearing one 19th century member of London's Travellers' Club advising another on a forthcoming journey.'
Philip Glazebrook, Author of Journey to Kars: A Modern Traveller in Ottoman Lands

'Murray's Handbooks were less visually appealing than Baedeker's guidebooks, but they contained far more detailed physical descriptions and historical learning.'
Edward Mendelson, Professor of English, Columbia University

The soft, red covered Murray's have become much sought after collector's items. With their fine maps and interesting recommendations they are listed by antiquarian booksellers with a value of up to £750!

Competition for a burgeoning guidebook market was provided by the Baedeker Guides, first published in 1846, and later by the Blue Guide Series with others quickly following suit.

- 1843: Lord Dalhousie started thinking about connecting India by railway.
- 16 April 1853: first train on Indian soil ran in Bombay from Bori Bunder to Thane.
- 1881: first hill railway to Darjeeling opened.
- 1888: Bombay Victoria Terminus built.
- 1999: Darjeeling hill railway declared world heritage site by UNESCO.
- 1999: Delhi Main Station gains place in *Guinness Book of World Records* for having the largest Route Relay Inter-locking System with 11,000 relays allowing for up to 1,122 signalled movements.
- Longest railway journey: Jammu Tawi to Kanyakumari, 3,751km on the Himsagar Express (around 66 hours).
- Longest railway platform in the world: Kharagpur – 2,733ft.
- Shortest station name: Ib, near Jharsuguda on the Howrah-Nagpur main line (South Eastern Railway).
- Longest station name: Venkatanarasim-harajuvariapeta (Halt) on the Arakkonam-Renigunta section of the Southern Railway.
- Longest run (time): The Himsagar Express. However, during British rule there used to be a Mangalore-Peshawar train, which took about 104 hours (in 1930). This is longer than the Orient Express which took about 60 hours between Paris and Istanbul), but it of course pales into insignificance next to the Trans-Siberian Express which takes about 170 hours (even today) between Moscow and Vladivostok.
- Fastest train: The highest speed ever touched by a train in India is 184km/h in 2000, when the LHB Alstom passenger coaches were under-going speed trials (on the Delhi-Ghaziabad route). The locomotive used was a WAP-5.
- Least punctual train: The Guwahati Express from Guwahati to Trivandrum. The train is booked to make its journey in 71 hours and 25 minutes, but the average delay on a trip is about 20 hours, with the train often showing up more than a day late. In 1995, the *Times of India* claimed the train had not run on time even once in its (then) 10-year existence! It preserved this distinction into the late 1990s, but is now reported to be running fairly punctually.
- Longest tunnel: The 6.5-km Karbude tunnel between Bhoke and Ukshi.
- Longest bridge: The Godavari bridge near Rajahmundry (a road-rail mixed traffic bridge, a little over 5km).
- Tallest bridge: The 64m-high bridge on the Panval river (Konkan Railway). The 420m-long bridge was the first one built in India using the incremental launching technique.

Tired of the same old vacation rounds?

Then come to HAWAII~this time!

As the tide rolled in, the Olympic organisers began to reconsider the wisdom of introducing beach pole-vaulting to the games

PIE IN THE SKY

One Lancashire couple never travel without one particular item: a 30-year-old meat pie. 'Pie' has been with the couple on their journeys around the world, managing to take in the sights at Las Vegas five times, Barbados four times, and most of Europe, Kuwait and the Falkland Islands, amassing a total distance of 500,000 miles. It originated as a joke when the couple's neighbour, a baker, gave them a pie that had been left in the oven over night. Pie was introduced into the family and soon began accompanying them on their travels. The couple always send a postcard from Pie to Holland's Pies, the bakers where it was born.

ROCK THE WORLD

Killer earthquakes

Date	Place	Richter Scale	Number killed
27/07/1976	Tangshan, China *164,000 injured*	7.5	255,000–655,000
01/09/1923	Kanto, Japan *The 'Great Tokyo Fire'*	7.9	143,000
05/10/1948	Ashgabat, Turkmenistan	7.3	110,000
28/12/1908	Messsina, Italy *Created a tsunami*	7.2	70,000–100,000
31/05/1970	Peru	7.9	66,000
30/05/1935	Quetta, Pakistan	7.5	30,000–60,000
26/12/2003	Bam, Iran *30,000 injured*	6.6	30,000
12/07/1988	Spitak, Armenia	6.8	25,000
19/09/1985	Michoacan, Mexico	8,0	9,500–30,000
26/01/2001	Gujara, India *166,836 injured*	7.7	20,005
08/17/1999	Izmit, Turkey *50,000 injured, 500,000 homeless*	7.6	17,118
22/05/1960	Chile *Strongest ever recorded in Chile*	9.5	4,000–5,000

DISTINCTIVE DWELLINGS

Cave hotel, Tunisia

It's not only *Star Wars* fans who'll be awed by the Hotel Sidi Driss. One of 'les Troglodytes' (traditional underground cave dwellings) is the Sidi Driss used as the location of Luke Skywalker's home in the original *Star Wars* film.

A typical Berber dwelling, the hotel has a central courtyard dug deep in the earth, surrounded by tunnels that lead to cave bedrooms and a cave restaurant.

62 *Percentage of travellers who say they become stressed over ensuring 'that every day is packed with activities'*

Vital travel information

The UK
18 international airports
22 domestic airports
10,497 miles of railway
231,106 miles of road
59.2 million inhabitants
I say, old chap, where can I water my camel?

Denmark
1 international airport
10 domestic airports
1,966 miles of railway
44,486 miles of road
5.3 million inhabitants
Der hvor kunne jeg vand mig kom?

Colombia
12 international airports
over 80 smaller landing strips
2,053 miles of railway
68,354 miles of road
44.2 million inhabitants
¿Dónde puedo regar yo mi camello?

Haiti
1 international airport
1 domestic airport and four smaller airfields
No railways
2,585 miles of road
8.3 million inhabitants
Où peux-j'arroser mon chameau?

Vanuatu
1 international airport
28 domestic airports
No railway
664 miles of road
212,000 inhabitants
Où peux-j'arroser mon chameau?

Jamaica
2 international airports
4 domestic airports
169 miles of railway
11,620 miles of road
2.6 million inhabitants
Where can I water my camel, man?

WHO GOES WHERE?

Visitors by year

Algeria	1 million	*60% French 14% Italians*
Australia	2.5 million	*24% Japanese 19% other Asian*
China	4 million	*27% Japanese 13% USA*
France	70 million	*23% German 14% UK*
India	1.7 million	*14% British 13% Bangladeshis*
Israel	2.2 million	*23% USA 11% French*
Italy	20 million	*30% German 10% French*
Jamaica	1 million	*67% USA 14% Canadian*
Japan	3.5 million	*24% Korean 20% Taiwanese*
Russia	3 million	*17% Chinese 16% Finnish*
UK	18.5 million	*15% USA 13% French*
USA	45.6 million	*43% Canadian 19% Mexican*

Number, in millions, of travellers who use Heathrow annually, serving approximately 170 destinations

TRAVELLING IN DISGUISE

John Simpson (1944–), the BBC's World Affairs Editor, has earned a reputation as one of the world's most experienced and authoritative journalists, in a BBC career spanning more than 30 years. He has reported from more than 100 countries across the globe, from 30 war zones, and has interviewed numerous world leaders. His most recent and demanding assignment was reporting from Afghanistan during the fall of Kabul. He was the first western journalist to get behind enemy lines in Taliban-controlled Afghanistan, before the war started. He arrived on the back of a truck, disguised as a woman dressed in a blue burkha. Other close shaves include being attacked with poisonous gas in the Gulf, dodging the bullets in Tiananmen Square and being punched by former British Prime Minister Harold Wilson. When asked about his incessant travelling, he quotes Sir Richard Burton: 'Starting in a hollowed log of wood – some thousand miles up a river, with an infinitesimal prospect of returning, I ask myself, "Why?" and the only echo is, "Damned fool! The Devil drives".'

TRAVEL NOTES

But to the man who would see for himself a country as it was left by the Creator before the hand of man has touched it – who will volun- tarily put himself back many generations to live for a while the life of his more primitive ancestors; who will care to live with the sky as his boundary and to sleep with the stars for a roof, as, with his feet stretched to the camp fire he thinks of far-off home and distant scenes, whilst ever and anon the stillness of the night is broken by the bark of the fox or the cry of some wandering puma seeking his prey – to him I can offer a vast field and scope for his wanderings, a life free for a short while from the daily worries and conventionalities of civilisation, where his time and his way are his own, to choose how he will and to go where he will.

WO Campbell, Victorian adventurer
Through Patagonia (1901)

QUOTE UNQUOTE

Sir, Saturday morning, although recurring at regular and well-foreseen intervals, always seems to take this railway by surprise.
WS GILBERT, lyricist, in a letter to the station-master at
Baker Street, on the Metropolitan line

AMONG THE WORST IN-FLIGHT FILMS OF ALL TIME

Apollo 13 – 1995
Airplane – 1980
And I Alone Survived – 1978
Angel Flight Down – 1996
Back from Eternity – 1956
The Concorde Affair – 1980
Crash – 1978
Crash Landing – 1958
Crisis in Mid-air – 1979
Panic in the Skies – 1996
Skyjacked – 1972
Shootdown – 1988
Terror in the Sky – 1971

When Charlie's Angels *(2000) is shown as an in-flight movie, airlines remove the opening scene of the angels retrieving a bomb from a 747, opening the emergency door, and parachuting out.*

WHICH HAT?

When entering a temple or a shrine, or even if you're just braving the elements, a well-prepared traveller should always have a hat on standby. A strong canvas hat with a wide brim is good for all weathers, but will need some kind of tie to stop it flying off in strong winds. If you buy it slightly too big, you can line the top with a handkerchief to make it warmer. Line the band with the same handkerchief to act as a sweatband when the weather's hot.

FANTASTIC FESTIVITIES

Day of the Dead, Mexico, *November*
El Dia De Los Muertos is the day of the dead in Mexico. This annual festival takes place on the 1st and 2nd of November (All Saints Day and All Souls Day), but rather than a simple day of mourning, it's a day of celebration with people preparing their favourite foods for absent friends. A traditional offering is the *pan de muerto*, which is a rich coffee cake decorated with meringues that resemble bones, skull-shaped sweets, marzipan death figures and skulls. The spirits are guided home by candles and flowers left on their graves and at 6pm the bells summoning the dead begin to ring, not stopping until sunrise.

CALL MY BLUFF, MARITIME STYLE

Which of the following definitions is the correct one for the following nautical names?

Davy Jones' Locker – the bottom of the ocean
1. A rather fierce pub owner named David Jones used to incapacitate helpless drinkers in his ale locker and then send them off on ships.
2. A derivation of the word devil.
3. Davy is a derivation of 'duffy', the West Indian term for ghost, Jones comes from Jonah and a locker is a valuable place to store things, so the whole phrase means that someone is safe with Duffy Jonah now.

Jolly Roger – a pirate flag featuring skeletons, dagger, cutlasses or bleeding hearts.
1. From the French term *joli rouge* meaning pretty red, to describe the blood-stained flag flown above pirate ships.
2. An Indian pirate called Ali Raja who flew a red flag, which English pirates called Alley Roger's flag. Alley could have been subsequently changed to jolly.
3. Old Roger was a common name for the devil and also an old English word for a vagabond or rogue.

Blue Peter – a blue flag with a white square in the centre indicating that the ship is ready to sail
1. It is a corruption of blue repeater, one of the British signal flags
2. It is the international signal flag for the letter P
3. Peter is a corruption of the French, *partir* (to leave)

Answer: Depends who you ask. Each of the above definitions is recognised as the true definition by at least one authority.

10 ROAD TRIP CLASSICS

Six days on the Road	Dave Dudley
Mustang Sally	Wilson Pickett
I Can See for Miles	The Who
Crossroads	Cream
Roadhouse Blues	Doors
Truckin'	Grateful Dead
Country Roads (Take Me Home)	John Denver
Take it Easy	Eagles
Life in the Fast Lane	Eagles
Cars	Gary Numan

An act of 1414, during the reign of Henry V, talks of the concept of 'Safe Conduct' with which one might travel abroad. Things became formalised when the Privy Council began granting passports in 1540. One of the earliest still in existence was issued on 18 June 1641, and was signed by Charles I. From 1644 to 1649, passes to British and foreign subjects were granted by the two Houses of Parliament. An order to the House of Commons dated 14 April 1649 directs that no pass should be granted to any person until he had first given an undertaking that he would not 'act, be aiding, assisting, advising or counselling against the Commonwealth'. Until the days of Charles II, the sovereign personally signed all British passports but in 1794, the Secretary of State took over the growing task. A record exists of all passports issued from that date.

By the outbreak of war in 1914 the price of a passport was 6d. The modern passport system really dates from this time as states started issuing passports as a means of distinguishing their citizens from those considered to be foreign nationals. The first modern UK passport was issued in 1915 when the British Nationality and *Status Aliens Act* 1914 came into force.

The old blue, 32-page British passport came into use as a result of a League of Nations International Conference on Passports after World War I. In the 1970s, increased overseas travel made security adaptation to passports necessary. Passports were issued for a single period of 10 years on 1 February 1968.

On 15 August 1988, the Passport Office began production of the new style burgundy red, machine-readable UK passport. This became known as the MRP while the former hard-backed blue passport became known as 'Old Blues' – though the traditional features of the Royal Coat of Arms and the written requirement to allow the holder free passage and protection were retained.

The machine-readable strip at the bottom of the details page enables immediate cross-referencing with immigration computers. The MRP also speeds up passage through frontier controls.

Some other security features of the new style passports are:
• A digitally-printed facial image of the holder, instead of a glued in photograph.
• The holder's signature is digitally captured onto the passport.
• The personal identification page is protected by a clear laminate, which incorporates a transparent optically variable device that protects the portrait.

Today, approximately five million British passports are issued every year in the UK.

GREEN TRAVELLING

Travelling is more popular than ever, and with the proliferation of cheap and easy travel, people are visiting many far flung corners of the globe. In 2002, almost 700 million people travelled worldwide. This has a huge impact on the environment. Air travel causes huge CO_2 emissions and airport expansion issues, to name just a couple. On the other hand, tourism can provide valuable income, jobs and foreign exchange to countries and communities that would otherwise struggle economically. So the answer for the concerned traveller would seem to be travel, but be aware of the impact you are having.

Some organisations that can help green travellers plan a guilt-free holiday are:

www.responsibletravel.com
www.tourismconcern.org.uk
www.tearfund.org

QUOTE UNQUOTE

Never, never be such a fool as to go up a mountain… men still ascend eminences… and descending, say they have been delighted. But it is a lie. They have been miserable the whole day.
WM THACKERAY, novelist

JUNGLE BOOK OF SURVIVAL

Insects find the saltiness of sweat attractive. Cover up well, especially sweaty places like your armpits and your groin. If ever you disturb a nest of bees or hornets, run!

When camping, keep clothing and boots off the ground to stop snakes and insects nesting in them. Always shake well before putting them back on.

If you find a hairy caterpillar climbing up your arm, brush it off in the direction it is climbing to stop any of its hairs sticking in your skin, which causes an irritating reaction.

Mosquitoes are especially active at dawn and dusk. Cover your face, head and hands as well as the rest of your body to protect yourself from them. In camp, a smoky fire will help keep all insects away.

Don't wash with soap: it removes natural oils in the skin, which act as a natural barrier to water and germs. Save soap for when you need clean hands, such as when administering first aid – soap is a better antiseptic than iodine, which will destroy skin as well as germs.

Percentage of all inbound arrivals to the US who come on the Visa Waive Program, meaning they can stay for 90 days without a visa

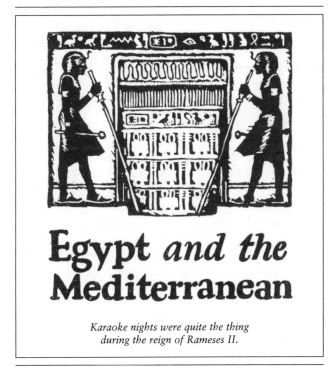

Egypt *and the* Mediterranean

Karaoke nights were quite the thing during the reign of Rameses II.

LEFT OR RIGHT?

When in 1923 Nova Scotia decided to change their driving habits from left to right, car owners put stickers on their windscreens to convince people aiming for a head on collision that they were driving on the right hand side of the road. However, it wasn't quite as easy to retrain the oxen who had been trained to walk on the left. So many oxen were involved in accidents, beef prices plummeted, and 1923 became known as the 'year of free beef'.

TRAVEL TEASERS

What links Argentina, Australia, Botswana, Brazil, Chile, Madagascar, Mozambique, Namibia, Paraguay and South Africa?
Answer on page 153

SURVIVED THE AGES

Hadrian's Wall, Northern England

Despite the Romans victorious invasion of southern and central England, they were unable to conquer the northern tribes. In 122 AD, Emperor Hadrian had a massive defence fortification built from Newcastle to Carlisle to effectively 'divide and rule' the peoples of England. The remaining wall presents a significant testimony to the power of the Roman Empire.

Lake Lugu, Yunnan, China

Living on the nearly inaccessible idyllic Lake Lugu in the Eastern Himalayas, the Mosuo peoples represent the last matriarchy in Asia. Here, it is the women who own and inherit property, and run the businesses.

Oasis of Siwa, Egypt

Some 2,300 years ago, Alexander the Great came to Siwa, a luscious oasis, to consult the oracle at the Temple of Ammon. The Temple built atop a rocky hill, still dominates the town, surrounded by a mud-brick minaret and palm-shaded paths.

Palmyra, Syria

One of the richest cities of antiquity, Palmyra served as a trading post for Arab camel caravans on the Silk Trading Route that linked the East and the West. The city was built on the Roman model, with an array of grand avenues, colonnades, and fountains. It was home to Queen Zenobia, the woman who almost succeeded in supplanting Rome, but was captured in chains of gold, ending Palmyra's glory in 272 AD.

Taj Mahal, Agra, India

The Taj Mahal is a testimony of the Mughal Empire's greatness during the 17th century. It took 20,000 men 20 years to build this beautiful marble mausoleum, in honour of Empress Mumtaz Mahal. Skilled craftsmen and precious stones for its interior were recruited from Europe through China for creating a 'structure that evoked paradise itself'.

DISTINCTIVE DWELLINGS

Tented safari lodge, Zimbabwe

The roar of lions, trumpeting of elephants and chattering of monkeys can all be heard through the canvas walls of your tented rooms when staying at a wilderness lodge in Africa. The comfortable walk-in tents of Linkwasha Tented Camp, in Hwange Park, Zimbabwe, are set off the ground on teak platforms, and linked by raised walkways.

They had crossed the Sewaliks and the half-tropical Doon, left Mussoorie behind them, and headed north along the narrow hill-roads. Day after day they struck deeper into the huddled mountains, and day after day Kim watched the lama return to a man's strength. Among the terraces of the Doon he had leaned on the boy's shoulder, ready to profit by wayside halts. Under the great ramp to Mussoorie he drew himself together as an old hunter faces a well-remembered bank, and where he should have sunk exhausted swung his long draperies about him, drew a deep double-lungful of the diamond air, and walked as only a Hillman can. Kim, plains-bred and plains-fed, sweated and panted astonished. 'This is my country,' said the lama. 'Beside Such-zen, this is flatter than a rice-field' and with steady, driving strokes from the loins he strode upwards. But it was on the steep downhill marches, three thousand feet in three hours, that he went utterly away from Kim, whose back ached with holding back, and whose big toe was nigh cut off by his grass sandal-string. Through the speckled shadow of the great deodar-forests; through oak feathered and plumed with ferns; birch, ilex, rhododendron, and pine, out on to the bare hillsides; slippery sunburnt grass, and back into the woodland's coolth again, till oak gave way to bamboo and palm of the valley, he swung untiring.

At first they breathed temperately upon the travellers, winds good to meet when one crawled over some gigantic hogback; but in a few days, at a height of nine or ten thousand feet, those breezes bit; and Kim kindly allowed a village of hillmen to acquire merit by giving him a rough blanket-coat. The lama was mildly surprised that any one should object to the knife-edged breezed which had cut the years off his shoulders.

'These are but the lower hills, chela. There is no cold till we come to the true Hills.'

'Air and water are good, and the people are devout enough, but the food is very bad,' Kim growled; 'and we walk as though we were mad – or English. It freezes at night, too.'

'A little, maybe; but only enough to make old bones rejoice in the sun. We must not always delight in the soft beds and rich food.'

'We might at the least keep to the road.'

Rudyard Kipling, *Kim*

QUOTE UNQUOTE

Travelling is almost like talking with men of other centuries.
RENE DESCARTES, French philosopher

BEEN THERE, DONE THAT

Western explorers who were the first to...

**Round the Cape of
Good Hope**
Bartolomeu Diaz
Portuguese explorer
1488

Cross the Sahara
Dixon Denham and
Hugh Clapperton
English explorers
1822–23

Explore the Zambesi River
David Livingstone
Scottish explorer
1851

Explore China
Marco Polo
Italian traveller
c.1272

Explore the Amazon River
Francisco Orellana
Spanish explorer
1541

**Explore Australia (first
European to reach the area)**
Abel Janszoon Tasman
Dutch navigator
1642

Cross Australia
John McDouall Stuart
Scottish explorer
1862

Cross the Antarctic Circle
James Cook
English navigator
1773

**Reach the North Pole
(controversial)**
Robert E Peary
American explorer
1909

Reach the South Pole
Roald Amundsen
Norwegian explorer
1911

TRAVEL NOTES

The Worldly Hope men set their Hearts upon
Turns Ashes – or it prospers; and anon,
Like Snow upon the Desert's dusty Face
Lighting a little hour or two – is gone.
Edward Fitzgerald, *The Rubaiyat of Omar Khayyam*

TRAVEL TIPS

It can be difficult to enter some countries, if another country has
stamped your passport. The US, for example, is notoriously difficult
for visitors arriving from Cuba. Find out before you enter a country
if their stamp might impede your travels later and if so, ask
NICELY if they wouldn't mind stamping a piece of paper instead.

HOTEL HEISTS

Items hotels expect their guests will take:
Soaps • Shower caps • Shampoos • Stationery
Sewing kits • Tea bags • Coffee sachets

**Items that hotels really didn't want their guests to take,
but they have done nonetheless:**
Towels – the most commonly stolen item
Pillows • Bedspreads • Bed sheets • Blankets
Bathroom sinks • Reclining chairs • Safe deposit boxes
Ashtrays • Pictures and wall hangings
Televisions and video players
Irons and ironing boards
A six and a half foot high ficus tree

- The American Hotel and Lodging Association estimates that theft in hotel rooms costs the US leisure industry US$100 million every year.
- Holiday Inn loses 560,000 towels a year.
- One in five Americans have taken a hotel towel.
- A study of British hoteliers revealed that women are more likely to steal a towel than men: 66% of women admitted to a theft whereas only 59% of men admit their involvement in such a crime.

SURVIVAL TIPS

Stranded on a desert island?
- Most seaweeds are edible but avoid any that are blue green and growing in fresh or stagnant water as are extremely poisonous.
- Avoid all filter feeders such as mussels as they concentrate toxins especially in the summer months.
- Avoid cone shells in the tropics as they can shoot out a poisonous barb, some of which are sufficiently toxic to kill a man.
- In a survival situation, cook all shellfish.
- Avoid going into the water barefoot as you might tread on poisonous spiny animals.
- When eating crab make sure it is cooked and that you've removed the lungs or 'dead men' as these are poisonous.
- Try and fish from the windward side of an island; the fish in a lagoon are often poisonous varieties or their eating habits cause them to be toxic.
- Coconuts provide food and water but too much coconut is a powerful purgative, especially the very young green or old brown nuts. Eat and drink in moderation.

After two years of training he went to sea, and entering the regions so well known to his imagination, found them strangely barren of adventure. He made many voyages. He knew the magic monotony of existence between sky and water: he had to bear the criticism of men, the exactions of the sea, and the prosaic severity of the daily task that gives bread – but whose only reward is in the perfect love of the work. This reward eluded him. Yet he could not go back, because there is nothing more enticing, disenchanting, and enslaving than the life at sea. Besides, his prospects were good. He was gentlemanly, steady, tractable, with a thorough knowledge of his duties; and in time, when yet very young, he became chief mate of a fine ship, without ever having been tested by those events of the sea that show in the light of day the inner worth of a man, the edge of his temper, and the fibre of his stuff; that reveal the quality of his resistance and the secret truth of his pretences, not only to others but also to himself.

Joseph Conrad, *Lord Jim*

¿HABLAS ESPAÑOL?

• There are 21 Spanish-speaking countries in the world: Argentina, Bolivia, Chile, Colombia, Costa Rica, Cuba, Dominica Republic, Ecuador, El Salvador, Equatorial Guinea, Guatemala, Honduras, Mexico, Nicaragua, Panama, Paraguay, Peru, Puerto Rico, Spain, Uruguay and Venezuela.

• The total number of Spanish-speaking people in the world is 373.3 million. Mexico has the largest population with 93.7 million, the smallest is Equatorial Guinea with 0.5 million people.

• Brazil, whose 170 million inhabitants speak Portuguese, accounts for nearly 50% of the South American population.

AKA

Nicknames of cities round the world

Paris, France	*City of Lights*
Rome, Italy	*City of the Seven Hills*
Manila, Philippines	*Pearl of the Orient*
Prague, Czech Republic	*City of a Hundred Spires*
Salzburg, Austria	*Festival City*
Berlin, Germany	*Millennium City*

In 1892, aged 30, Mary Kingsley set off for West Africa where she planned to research African religions and laws in order to finish a book her uncle, Charles Kingsley, had left unfinished at his death. Between 1893 and 1894 she travelled to Angola, Nigeria, and the islands of Fernando Po, collecting all sorts of booty which was gratefully accepted by the Natural History section of the British Museum. She also travelled in the Congo and previously unexplored parts of Gabon.

She wrote prolifically, always expressing her deep affection for black African people. Of the Fan people whom she encountered during her ascent of the Ogowe river in Gabon, in an expedition of 1894, she wrote in *Travels in West Africa*: 'I must not forget to mention the other member of our party, a Fan gentleman with the manners of a duke and the habits of a dustbin. He came with us, quite uninvited by me, and never asked for any pay: I think he only wanted to see the fun, and drop in for a fight if there was one going on, and to pick up the pieces generally. He was evidently a man of some importance, from the way the others treated him; and moreover he had a splendid gun, with a gorilla skin sheath for its lock, and ornamented all over its stock with brass nails. His costume consisted of a small piece of dirty rag round his loins; and whenever we were going through dense undergrowth, or wading a swamp, he wore that filament tucked up scandalously short. Whenever we were sitting down in the forest having one of our nondescript meals, he always sat next to me and appropriated the tin. Then he would fill his pipe, and turning to me with the easy grace of aristocracy, would say what may be translated as "My dear Princess, could you favour me with a Lucifer?" I used to say, "My dear Duke, charmed, I'm sure," and give him one ready lit.'

Kingsley had her views about women's attire, too: 'One should not go about in Africa in something of which one would be ashamed at home. I hasten to assure you that I never ever wear a masculine collar and tie, and as for encasing the more earthward extremities of my anatomy in – you know what I mean – well, I would rather perish on the public scaffold!'

QUOTE UNQUOTE

Think of your life in nature – daily to be shown matter, to come in contact with it – rocks, trees, wind in our cheeks! the solid earth! the actual world! the common sense! Contact! Contact!
HENRY DAVID THOREAU, writer and naturalist

TRAVEL TEASERS

A French plane carrying Spanish passengers from Germany to Canada crashes in the sea between Ireland and America. Where do they bury the survivors?

Answer on page 153

DEAD SEA? DYING SEA

The Dead Sea is landlocked between Jordan and Israel at the lowest point of the earth, some 400m below sea level. Bathers can enjoy the strange sensation of floating unaided in the extremely salty water. But maybe not for much longer. The popular tourist attraction is in fact shrinking. It is estimated that the water level has dropped by more than 130ft in the last 50 years and it is still dropping by as much as three feet per year in recent times. The area of the sea is now a third less than it was a century ago. It is thought that the water is disappearing as a result of commercial siphoning.

You couldn't storm up and down the Dead Sea exhibiting a punishing crawl: the water's so salty you'd burn your eyes. There are signs all around the bathing places warning people to keep the water out of their eyes. The other phenomenon which isn't often mentioned is its stink produced by its sulphurous mud (which is supposed to have all sorts of beneficial qualities).

THE SIGNS AREN'T GOOD

In a Tokyo Hotel:
Is forbidden to steal hotel towels please. If you are not a person to do such thing is please not to read notis.

Two signs in a Bucharest hotel lobby:
The lift is being fixed for the next day. During that time we regret that you will be unbearable.
To move the cabin, push button for wishing floor. If the cabin should enter more persons, each one should press a number of wishing floor. Driving is then going alphabetically by national order.

In a Paris hotel elevator:
Please leave your values at the front desk.

In a hotel in Athens:
Visitors are expected to complain at the office between the hours of 9 and 11am daily.

In a Yugoslavian hotel:
The flattening of underwear with pleasure is the job of the chambermaid.

THE ANCIENT WONDERS OF THE WORLD

The list of the Seven Wonders of the Ancient World was originally compiled around the 2nd century BC although the first reference is found in Herodotus' *Histories* in the 5th century BC. The list we know today was compiled during the Middle Ages despite hardly any of the Wonders actually surviving as long as this.

Pyramids of Giza
A gigantic stone structure near the ancient city of Memphis. It is the only Wonder still standing, despite being the oldest, having been built around the year 2560 BC.

Hanging Gardens of Babylon
The gardens in question were connected with a palace built on the banks of the River Euphrates, near Baghdad by King Nebuchadnezzar II.

Statue of Zeus at Olympia
An enormous statue of the Greek god of gods, carved by sculptor Pheidias at the ancient town of Olympia, on the west coast of modern Greece. The statue ended its life after the Olympic games were banned in 391 AD as Pagan practices by the Emperor Theodosius I.

Temple of Artemis at Ephesus
A beautiful temple in the ancient city of Ephesus near the modern town of Selcuk, in Turkey. It was erected in honour of the Greek goddess of hunting around 550 BC. On the night of 21 July 356 BC, Herostratus burned the temple to the ground.

Mausoleum of Maussollos at Bodrum in modern Turkey
A fascinating tomb constructed in 350 BC for King Maussollos, Persian *satrap* (provincial governor) of Caria in the city of Bodrum on the Aegean Sea, in South-west Turkey. The tomb survived for 16 centuries until an earthquake caused damage to the roof and colonnade.

Colossus of Rhodes
This Wonder was a Colossus of Helios the sun god erected at the entrance to the harbour in Rhodes. The construction of the Colossus took 12 years and was finally finished in 282 BC. For years, the statue stood guard at the harbour entrance, until a strong earthquake hit Rhodes in about 226 BC. The city was badly damaged, and the Colossus was broken at its weakest point (the knee) and it fell.

The Lighthouse at Alexandria
A lighthouse, built by the Ptolemies on the island of Pharos, off the coast of their capital city, to ensure a safe return to the harbour for sailors navigating the difficult waters. It was also the tallest building on earth at the time and was conceived around 290 BC by Ptolemy Soter. It used fire at night and reflected sunlight during the day. The lighthouse was ruined by earthquakes over several centuries.

ENGLAND
the daily pageant

Lionel knew he could conquer the world, now that he had successfully cloned an army of vicious beefeaters.

QUOTE UNQUOTE

I am not an empire builder, I am not a missionary, I am not truly a scientist. I merely want to return to Africa and continue my wanderings.
JOSEPH THOMSON, writer

78 *Percentage of people between 35 and 45 who argue with their partner over where to holiday or travel*

ON TRAVELLING IN THE HIMALAYAS

'No-one ever travelled far during the monsoon if he could help it.' *Eric Shipton*

'I felt I could go on like this for ever, that life had little better to offer than to march day after day in an unknown country to an unattainable goal.' *HW Tilman*

'The art of Himalayan travel... is the art of being bold enough to enjoy life now.' *WH Murray*

'The pull of Everest was stronger for me than any force on earth.' *Tenzing Norgay*

'Mountains are fountains, not only of rivers and fertile soil, but of men. Therefore we are all, in some sense, mountaineers, and going to the mountains is going home.' *John Muir*

'The journey should be carefully planned beforehand, especial study being given to the matter of gradients.' *Karl Baedeker*

'At the end of the fight is a tombstone white with the name of the late deceased
And the epitaph drear: A fool lies here who tried to hustle the East.' *Rudyard Kipling*

'Those with weak hearts, palpitations, and so forth must, of course, avoid ascents altogether.' *Karl Baedeker*

'The whole of Nepal is like a pretty woman, with a blush ever ready to erupt.' *The Times of India*

'And the wildest dreams of Kew are the facts of Kathmandu.' *Rudyard Kipling*

A RUM FELLOW

Captain Morgan, a familiar face to rum drinkers, has adorned thousands of bottles of original spiced rum. Unlike many brand characters, however, Captain Morgan did actually exist.

Sir Henry Morgan (1635-1688) was essentially a pirate, but a pirate with some very influential friends. Based in Jamaica, he was able to take advantage of the fact that Britain had a valuable province but no way of defending it. The Crown back in London were at the time relying on privateers and buccaneers to protect the island. Although King Charles II claimed to not know about this state-funded piracy, Morgan was able to grow wealthy from just such a role. He carried on with plundering and looting until he was arrested and taken back to London. However he was soon knighted and reinstated to his duties in Jamaica where he continued to patrol the Caribbean until his death in 1688.

FANTASTIC FESTIVITIES

Kattenwoensdog, Ypres, Belgium, *May*

Over 200 years ago, this Belgian town was overrun with mice. To solve the problem, the resourceful locals brought in cats. However, once the mice were dealt with, the locals had a self-induced cat plague to deal with. Rather than finding an animal willing to hunt down the felines the residents decided to take matters into their own hands, literally. They caught the cats and threw them off the top of a tall tower. Today the festival still involves tabby tossing, but of the fluffy and fake variety. So, if you have an aversion to cats then perhaps you should head to the belfry of the Cloth Hall on the second Sunday in May. Every other year, the cat hurling is complemented with parades celebrating famous cats.

FASTEST RAIL JOURNEYS

	Distance		Speed	
Journey, *Country*	(km)	(miles)	(km/h)	(mph)
1. Hiroshima–Kokura, *Japan*	192	119.3	261.8	162.7
2. Valence–Avignon, *France*	129.7	80.6	259.4	161.2
3. Brussels Midi–Valence, *Belgium and France*	831.3	516.5	242.1	150.4
4. Madrid–Seville, *Spain*	470.5	292.4	209.1	129.9
5. Stendal–Wolfsburg, *Germany*	76.2	47.3	190.4	118.3
6. York–Stevenage, *UK*	258	160.3	182.8	113.6
7. Skovde–Sodertalje, *Sweden*	277	172.1	173.1	107.6
8. Rome–Florence, *Italy*	261	162.2	166.6	103.5
9. Baltimore–Wilmington, *USA*	110.1	68.4	165.1	102.6
10.Salo–Karjaa, *Finland*	53.1	33	151.7	94.3

MIND HOW YOU GO

The most dangerous road in the world, according to the Association for Safe International Travel, is in Bolivia. This popular tourist trail starts at 4,700m high in the mountains and descends 3,600m over 60 miles to the rainforest and jungle below. A vehicle, usually a truck or passenger bus, goes off the side of the road about once a fortnight.

The road, which links La Paz and the Yungas, is mostly made up of a one-lane dirt track with regular intervals cut into the cliff. If two vehicles meet then one has to reverse until there is room to get past. The Andean drivers of the buses follow a variety of rituals to keep them safe on the death-defying trail, including splashing their tyres with alcohol to bless the vehicle. To increase their chances of making the journey alive they also make offerings of coca leaves and build little rock cairns.

TRAVEL NOTES

I must have been about four years old when Russia took hold of me with giant hands...

The traveller had come to rest in the rocking-chair. The clumsy folds of his great fur-lined overcoat stood round him like a box, while a number of scarves tangled under his chin. His tight-skinned Chinese-yellow face seemed to glow, incandescent, in the light of the nursery fire where we made beef-dripping toast together. Even this warming occupation could not persuade him to remove his overcoat.

'You'll catch your death of cold when you go out,' my nurse would always say.

'Not after Siberia,' the traveller would always reply. It was a ritual.

Of the lands he had known, his own, Russia, seemed to me the most fabulous. He was from Moscow, 'a Muscovite,' he said, but later I was to learn he was of Tartar blood; and unmistakably, the Ta-tze or Mongol hordes had stamped their imprint on his strange countenance. The dark slit eyes, the pointed ears, the bald, Chinese-yellow skull, the slight, yet cruel smile which sometimes passed across his usually impassive face – all these spoke of Asia, of the Golden Horde, and the limitless horizons of Central Asia, where he roamed, in spirit, and in fact.

Lesley Blanch, *Journey Into the Mind's Eye*

OLD ROAD TO CHINA

If you were hitching a camel ride from Syria to China, around 1425, this is the route you would take:

Aleppo, Damascus, Babylon,
Selencia, Ecbatane, Merv, Bukhara,
Samarkand, Kashgar, Yarkand, Cherchen,
Dunhuang, Changian

LEFT OR RIGHT?

Contrary to popular tradition jousters always rode on the right carrying their lances with their strong right arms so that they could attack their opponents across their bodies on the left. The reason people used to drive on the left is that it's easier to control a horse with the right arm. If you were walking along pulling a cart you wouldn't want to be in the middle of the road, you'd put the horse there. You also mount and dismount a horse from the left because you'd wear your sword on you left side so you can draw it easily with your right arm. And if you were attacked on the road it would be easier if you were on the left for the same sword drawing reasons. Which is why we drive on the left.

Above all do not lose your desire to walk.
KIERKEGAARD, philosopher

THE 10 MOST POPULAR ADVENTURE TRAVELLING ACTIVITIES

1. Walking, hiking and trekking
2. Cycling
3. Cross-country skiing
4. Dog sledging
5. Horse riding
6. White-water rafting
7. Kayaking and Sea-kayaking
8. Mountaineering and climbing
9. Scuba Diving
10. Off-road Driving

HISTORIC HOLIDAYS

Shed the centuries

**Borobudur,
Jogjakarta, Indonesia**
In the middle of the Indonesian jungle sits the giant stupa, Borobudur, built during the 8th and 9th centuries. The shrine is arranged in nine terraces measuring 2.5km long, embellished by hundreds of Buddha statues and descriptive friezes.

Visby, Gotland, Sweden
Once a Stone Age sacrificial site, Visby was resettled by the Vikings in the 6th century. They used it as a base for trading routes to Asia and developed it into a perfect medieval stronghold. The 1350s saw a plague that killed more than 8,000 people, and although it was refurbished by the Germans, the Pearl of the Baltic or the City of Roses never regained its status.

**The Lascaux Cave,
Dordogne, France**
Accidentally discovered in 1940, this 15,000-year-old cave contains striking paintings of horses and wild oxen as well as the tools that the artists used. The original is now closed, but this testimony of the Stone Age can still be experienced in a replica nearby.

**Ryoangi Rock Garden,
Kyoto, Japan**
15th century Japanese culture is delicately portrayed in this *kare-sansui* (dry landscape) garden. Fifteen rocks are grouped in small islands on a sea of white gravel. The garden is a reflection of Zen Buddhism, indeed, only with enlightenment can one see the 15th-century rock.

HIGH ALTITUDE HUMOUR

A lot of people have been on an aeroplane. And a lot of people have heard the safety announcements just one too many times. Sometimes the airline staff make attempts to liven up these and other announcements by adding their own little touch. Here are some examples that have been heard or reported:

On a flight with a very 'senior' flight attendant crew: 'Ladies and gentlemen, we've reached cruising altitude and will be turning down the cabin lights. This is for your comfort and to enhance the appearance of your flight attendants.'

On landing: 'Please be sure to take all your belongings. If you're going to leave anything, please make sure it's something we'd like to have.'

'There may be 50 ways to leave your lover, but there are only four ways to leave the aircraft.'

'To operate your seat belt, insert the metal tab into the buckle, and pull tight. It works just like every other seat belt; and, if you don't know how to operate one, you probably shouldn't be out in public unsupervised.'

'In the event of a sudden loss of cabin pressure, masks will descend from the ceiling. Stop screaming, grab the mask, and pull it over your face. If you have a small child travelling with you, secure your mask before assisting with theirs. If you are travelling with more than one small child, pick your favourite.'

'Your seat cushions can be used for flotation; and in the event of an emergency water landing, please paddle to shore and take them with our compliments.'

'As you exit the plane, make sure to gather all of your belongings. Anything left behind will be distributed evenly among the flight attendants. Please do not leave children or spouses.'

And from the pilot during his welcome message: 'This airline is pleased to have some of the best flight attendants in the industry. Unfortunately, none of them are on this flight!'

Another flight attendant's comment on a less than perfect landing: 'We ask you to please remain seated as Captain Kangaroo bounces us to the terminal.'

TRAVEL TEASERS

Where in America?
NESOMTA
Answer on page 153

MURPHY'S LAWS FOR FREQUENT FLYERS

No flight ever leaves on time unless you are running late and need the delay to make the flight.

If you are running late for a flight, it will depart from the farthest gate within the terminal.

If you arrive very early for a flight, it inevitably will be delayed.

Flights never leave from Gate One at any terminal in the world.

If you must work on your flight, you will experience turbulence as soon as you touch pen to paper.

If you are assigned a middle seat, you can determine who has the seats on the aisle and the window while you are still in the boarding area. Just look for the two largest passengers.

Only passengers seated in window seats ever have to get up to go to the lavatory.

The crying baby on board the flight is always seated next to you.

The strength of the turbulence is directly proportional to the temperature of your coffee.

The less carry-on luggage space available on an aircraft, the more carry-on luggage passengers will bring aboard.

QUOTE UNQUOTE

Take only pictures, cast only shadows, leave only ripples of understanding as you travel the world.
DAVID BELLAMY, naturalist

HERO FOR HIRE

Travelling solo is not everyone's idea of a dream getaway. Some people prefer a good chinwag and a buddy to share the journey with. But what if your friends prefer popping to the corner shop rather than a 20-hour train ride across India or a hike through the Andes? Well, a new escort service for women has solved this problem by offering men for hire to share holidays and travels. For £3,000 the woman gets attention and pampering on demand for her trip. The agency was the brain child of ex-model Steve Jarsman from Perth who capitalised on women's desire for their boyfriends to be willing to join them round the world and fawn over them on the way. Escorts in Paradise hopes to bring women's desires for romantic travel and fantasy alive. Jarsman adds that: 'client's pay for an escorts's time. If a lady wants to take the relationship further, and 80% of them do, then that's between her and the escort.'

TRAVELLING IN DISGUISE

Sir Richard Francis Burton (1821–1890) was an explorer, linguist, diplomat, anthropologist, and a gifted writer. He wrote essays and books about everything he saw, and every place he visited, from Asia through Africa to South America. He discovered the source of the Nile, translated the *Kama Sutra* and the *Arabian Nights*, and was knighted by Queen Victoria. However, he is best known as a master of disguise. Starting as an undercover intelligence officer during the Sikh War, he perfected his ability in language and disguise. His most famous feat was infiltrating the Mecca and the Medina in 1853. Disguised as an Afghan physician, he was the first 'infidel' to kiss the Kaaba. He had to perform almost hourly minute ceremonials, in which, had he failed to pay attention to detail, he would have been torn to pieces. Unsatisfied with this victory, Burton set out to enter the forbidden Muslim city of Harar, in Somalia. All non-believers who had entered this city before him had been executed, and in this Burton became the first white man to enter and leave alive.

PASSPORT, TICKETS, CAMERA, KETCHUP...

Going away can be about the joy of different places and the experiencing of alien cultures and meeting new people. However, everyone can be prone to a little homesickness. But what if a call home or a photo of a loved one is not enough? Well, you can always take the next step and take a piece of home with you.

Travellers have admitted that they like to take a piece of Britain with them when they are in foreign climes. And what they take can say something about what people really like about 'home'.

More than anything people want to be reminded of British food. Often derided as the worst cuisine of the world, Brits can't get enough of it while travelling the globe. And while its hard to take fish and chips, a Sunday roast or even a chicken tikka masala, people are making do with what comes in handy rucksack sized containers. According to a recent survey, the item most people take with them is tomato ketchup. Teabags from home are a more expected addition to the packing, and what is nicer than a few biscuits with your cuppa? Cornflakes, marmite and baked beans also made the list.

COMIC TIMING

Can elephants run? The majestic beasts are accused of 'running' like Groucho Marx by John Hutchinson of Stanford University, California. However, even at top speed all four feet never leave the ground at once, which is, technically, walking.

OLD POSTER, NEW CAPTION

Three years after being allowed to paint her, Whistler was beginning to regret the deal he'd made with his mother.

TIME TRAVELLER CHECKS

We all know what we'd do if we had a time travel machine (besides fainting, shouting, jumping up and down etc), as Marty realised in *Back To The Future*: come back from the future with all the information you need to make a million.

When Andrew Carlssin turned a stock market investment of US$350 into a portfolio valued at more than US$800 million in two weeks, he was arrested by federal investigators. He explained, in his defence, that he had come back from the year 2256 when everyone knew that our era suffered one of the worst stock plunges in history. Apparently the Security and Exchange Commission didn't believe him. So now all he needs is the Doc to come and rescue him.

FRENCH FRIED

In 1950, French senator and former witch-doctor Victor Biaka-Boda travelled to the Ivory Coast, which he represented, to assess the electorate's concerns and drum up their support. They obviously liked the look of him because they ate him, but it's not clear whether he went down well.

DISTINCTIVE DWELLINGS

Floating luxury, Paris, France

Step on board La Vie en Rose, a luxury peniche, or riverboat, in the heart of Paris. Moored on the River Seine between the Ile St Louis and the Left Bank, La Vie en Rose is just upstream from Notre Dame cathedral. The floating hotel has a glass-walled sitting room and fully-fitted bathroom, but only one bedroom, making it the perfect hideaway for two.

A full breakfast is provided every morning, and teatime snacks await hungry travellers after a day spent sightseeing or shopping. And here's the sign of true extravagance – maid service not once, but twice a day. Truly a rosy existence, as the name implies.

SIGNS YOU'RE A SEASONED TRAVELLER

All your passport pages have been used up.

It's quicker to list the countries you haven't been to.

You have friends in countries your friends from home haven't even heard of.

You have been medically classified as resistant to all known diseases on account of all the immunisation injections you've received.

The travel supplement in the Sunday paper is more a trip down memory lane than an inspiration for your next holiday.

The staff at Heathrow know you by name.

You have enough frequent flier miles to get to the moon.

Your lifetime guaranteed rucksack is giving up the will to live.

You've written the equivalent of a small novel on the back of postcards.

You feel more comfortable when sleeping on a bunk bed in a room with 12 other people from eight different countries.

I'VE BEEN HERE BEFORE...

Many people dream of spending time in some far-away foreign place, but few imagine they have already lived in a country they've never set foot in. Jesper Bood, a 29-year-old Swedish man who had never been to Scotland, was hypnotised for a documentary about reincarnation and claimed to have lived in the East Lothian town of Dunbar in the 1860s. He was able to describe the town in amazing detail and drew a map of the town blindfolded.

NOT THE SHARPEST TRAVELLER IN THE BOX

Ever had one of those days where you have become convinced that the general public perhaps lack a little common sense? Workers at tourist information centres around the UK seem to have become entirely convinced that the general public have actually never been even remotely acquainted with common sense, general knowledge or indeed the ability to manage with daily life. The English Tourism Council and Visit Scotland have released a list of 'quirky' enquiries they have received over the years. Included on the list are such diverse questions as:

- Is Dorking something English people do?
- What time does the Lake District open?
- What time do the UFOs fly, where can we sit and watch them and would it be all right to bring a picnic?
- I understand there is a gorilla breeding establishment somewhere in the South of England. Please could you tell me where it is because I want to take my wife there as a surprise?
- What time does the 10.20am bus run?
- Can I change my English currency into Scottish currency?
- Exactly where on the map does the Scottish accent stop and the English one start?
- Can you give me a list of garages selling petrol between Stoke-on-Trent and Windsor?
- What day is the New Years Day Parade on?
- How does the snow get up on Ben Nevis?
- How do you get to Brigadoon?
- Where are the Northern Lights and what time do they get turned on?
- Is Fort William still alive?

Oh dear.

FANTASTIC FESTIVITIES

Skirt-lifting Festival, San Pablo de los Montes, Spain, *January*
It's the one date all the men in the town never forget, but still the women are not impressed, for this is the fiesta of St Paul – the day when men can go around lifting up girls' skirts without getting battered over the head for indecent behaviour. However, one unfortunate man is picked each year to be dressed as 'la Madre Cochina' (the Old Bat), tarted up, paraded and molested by all and sundry.

BON VOYAGE

If you don't want to say it in French...

Spanish..*El viaje bueno*
German ....*Gute Reise*
Italian ....*Buon viaggio*
Dutch...*Sloeg reis op*
Norwegian..*Bon sjøreise*
Portuguese ....*A viagem de bo*
Danish..*Heldig rejse*
Finnish ....*Iloinen matkustaa*
Welsh..*'N ddedwydd fordwya*
Latin...*Gauisus navigatio*

TRAVEL NOTES

The best way of travel, however, if you aren't in any hurry at all, if you don't care where you are going, if you don't like to use your legs, if you don't want to be annoyed at all by any choice of directions, is in a balloon. In a balloon, you can decide only when to start, and usually when to stop. The rest is left entirely to nature.

William Pène du Bois, *The Twenty-one Balloons.*

FREE WHEELING

So if you want to travel the world for a while, a long while, how on earth do you pay for it? You could always go for Ramon Stoppelenburg's way. The Dutch student simply asked people if they would be willing to put him up for the night as he passed through. His website www.letmestay-foraday.com led to an unexpectedly long trip around the world. Ramon received 3,577 invitations from 72 countries since setting off from his home in Zwoller in early 2001. In return for his accommodation he posts accounts of his travels on his website.

Ramon says that he had no idea what to expect when he established the site, although he thought that he would not get much further than his home town. The response was huge however and so off he went. He managed to travel for a year and a half without spending any money at all. Strangers helped him with accommodation and food and even with transport, sponsoring his travel and using their frequent flier miles to help him out. When that failed he hitchhiked. Just goes to show you what you can do with a little help from your friends. Or at least people you've never met but have visited your website.

If you want to send smoke signals first find a clearing in which to make your fire. Smoke will otherwise be hidden by the tree canopy. You could equally make a fire to send smoke signals from a raft on a river.

To make your fire you'll need to find dry tinder. The inside of standing dead wood will work well. So will dry bamboo and termites' nests.

In the jungle, it's very important to keep your feet covered to protect them from leeches, and flesh-eating chigoe and centipedes. Use bark or cloth to wrap legs from boots upwards to protect them.

Leeches do not have a painful bite so you might not notice when one attaches itself to you. To get rid of a leech use a dab of salt, the end of a cigarette or a match flame and it'll drop off: never pull a leech off the skin as you might leave the head behind, buried under your skin, and that will probably go septic.

The famous candiru is the tiny catfish which will, extremely rarely, swim up the urethra of someone peeing in a river. So, at the risk of stating the obvious... don't pee when you're standing deep in jungle water.

QUOTE UNQUOTE

The world, which is a curious sight
And very much unlike what people write
LORD BYRON, poet

NEVER THE TWAIN DID MEET

In 1867, Mark Twain took a Cook's tour to Europe and the Eastern Mediterranean, during which he wrote and dispatched pieces to the *Alta California*, a San Francisco paper which sponsored his trip. Twain's dispatches were collated and published in a book entitled *The Innocents Abroad or The New Pilgrims Progress*, a book which sold over 70,000 copies in its first year in print and which was the best selling of Twain's works while he was still alive. It was in another piece, entitled, *Europe and Elsewhere* published in 1923, that Twain said of the tour operator Thomas Cook:

'Cook has made travel simple, easy and a pleasure. He will sell you a ticket to any place on the globe. Cook is your banker everywhere. His clerks will answer all the questions you ask, and do it courteously. I recommend Cook's tickets and I do without embarrassment, for I get no commission. I do not know Cook.'

TALLEST HOTELS

The world's tallest hotels according to *The Top 10 of Everything 2004:*

	Storeys	Height
1. Jin Mao Tower, *Shanghai, China*	88	370m
Grand Hyatt occupies floors 53–87		
2. Shimao International Plaza, *Shanghai, China*	60	333m
A hotel will occupy 48 of its floors in 2004		
3. Baiyoke Tower 2, *Bangkok, Thailand*	89	309m
Baiyoke Sky Hotel occupies floors 22–74		
4. Burj Al Arab, *Dubai, UAE*	60	270m
5. Emirates Tower 2, *Dubai, UAE*	50	262m
6. Thai Wah Tower, *Bangkok, Thailand*	60	260m
7. Grand Duta Hyatt, *Kuala Lumpur, Malaysia*	60	243m
8. Four Seasons Hotel and Tower, *Miami, Florida*	54	241m
9. JR Central Towers, *Nagoya, Japan*	53	240m
10. Grand Gateway, *Shanghai, China*	52	233m

TRAVEL NOTES

In my days as a student, I once found myself standing in a rat-infested corridor inside the ironically named Golden Hotel in Peshawar, Pakistan. My face was hidden by a sizeable beard and I was wearing an ancient shalwar qumiz (sic) and Chitrali hat. After a month's trekking through the high peaks of the Hindu Kush, even some Afghans had started to mistake me for a local rather than the Rich Bastard I was.

The Golden Hotel's proprietor paused by a doorway and grinned, 'for you, my friend, I have the best room in all Peshawar.' He put his shoulder to the warped timbers and shoved. The door sprung open with a loud crack, and instantly half the ceiling collapsed onto a soiled mattress in the centre of the floor with an explosion of dust and dirty plaster. I looked at the pile of rubble and felt the few coins left in my pocket. I smiled thinly at my host, 'that'll do nicely,' I replied.

If Peshawar taught me one thing, it was that my days of low budget travel were well and truly over. I was sick of lugging around guide books that weighed almost as much as my backpack, and I no longer enjoyed sifting through their thousand characterless references to find that one half-decent restaurant or hotel. I also found it equally annoying to have to buy five different 'speciality' guides every time I wanted to discover all the finest things a place had to offer.

Simon Kelton, *Rich Bastard's Guide to Los Angeles*

A FEW USEFUL INTERNATIONAL HELLOS

Arabic	*Marhaba*
Cherokee	*O'siyo*
Farsi	*Salaam*
French	*Bonjour*
German	*Guten tag*
Greek	*Geia Sou*
Hawaiian	*Aloha*
Hebrew	*Shalom*
Hungarian	*Sziasztok*
Irish	*Dia duit*

THE BIG TWO

The first Lonely Planet guide was called *Across Asia on the Cheap*, the brainchild of Maureen and Tony Wheeler who put it together at their kitchen table. At the time it was groundbreaking as it was custom made for the newly emerging backpackers who wanted to travel all over the world. It was published in 1973 and sold 8,000 copies in just three months in Australia and New Zealand. Spurred on by their success, they set about writing the follow up, *South-East Asia on a Shoestring* in a back street hotel in Singapore. The series has developed a lot since then, selling more than 5.5 million books a year in 118 countries.

The name Lonely Planet actually came about from a misunderstanding. Tony thought that Joe Cocker was singing 'lonely planet' when he was really singing 'lovely planet' in 'Space Captain'. Which might have been a slightly nicer spin.

Rough Guides were started by disgruntled student Mark Ellingham who decided that his guidebook to Greece was a bit rubbish and that he could probably do a lot better. So, he got a typewriter and put together a guide with a group of friends. It came out in 1981 and offered an insight into politics, geography and contemporary life with an honest and practical approach to traveller's needs and the local area. The series now covers 200 destinations around the globe.

FIVE FEARS TO GET YOU TRAVELLING

Claustrophobia	enclosed spaces
Omatophobia, oikophobia	home
Ecophobia	home surroundings
Thaasophobia	sitting idle
Eremophobia	stillness

WHAT YOU DIDN'T PRESUME
ABOUT LIVINGSTONE

He was born in 1813 into a poor Scottish family and worked
in a cotton factory from the age of 10.

He never went to school.

Self taught he studied geology and botany as well as medicine until he
had enough knowledge to qualify for his medical diploma.

In 1840, he was sent by the Missionary Society of London to
Botswana not only to practise Evangelism but also to preach against
the slave trade which still existed with Arab traders from the North.

At first he didn't travel alone. In 1849, the party for his first
exploration included his wife, three children and several friends.

His various journeys made him the first European to cross southern
Africa from west to east.

TRAVEL TEASERS

A train leaves from New York City heading toward Los Angeles at
100mph. Three hours later, a train leaves from Los Angeles heading
toward New York City at 200mph. Assuming there are exactly
2,000 miles between Los Angeles and New York City. As they pass
each other, which train is closer to New York City?
Answer on page 153

FANTASTIC FESTIVITIES

Camel Wrestling Championship
Selcuk, Turkey, *January*
The Turkish answer to bullfights and cockfights, this involves getting
two bull camels in an arena and parading a young female to get them
feeling all macho. It's easy to tell when a bull is getting excited, as
milky saliva streams from their mouth and nostrils. However, the
bulls normally half-heartedly butt each other until one runs away –
and then ensures the excitement, as the crowd try to avoid a tonne of
camel which is headed their way.

Cheese Rolling
Gloucester, *end of May*
A seven pound lump of cheese is rolled down a 300 yard-high slope
at Cooper's Hill, with a gradient of 2 in 1. Contestants roll down
after it. Winner takes the cheese.

OLD POSTER, NEW CAPTION

Waking from her deep sleep, the Statue of Liberty realised she had floated straight up a Norwegian fjord.

THE WOMAN BEHIND THE MAN

When arctic and antarctic explorer Ranulph Fiennes' wife first suggested he go round the world from top to bottom instead of side to side he replied: 'no sane person even tries to do it. If it were possible it would have been done. All oceans have been crossed west to east, north to south, solo, on rafts, backwards and sideways. All major mountains have been climbed and all rivers travelled up to their source and back down again. People have gone round the world by horse, bicycle and probably by broomstick. They have parachuted from over 30,000ft and gone paddling to the deepest spots in the deepest seas. Quite apart from strolling around on the moon.'

She was unimpressed. 'You're saying it can't be done because it hasn't been done. Is that it? That's pathetic.'

QUOTE UNQUOTE

Nothing surprises foreigners so much as the numbers of our countrymen that travel. The Swiss in particular often ask me how it happened, and said our country must be very unhealthy that everyone was so eager to get out of it.
WILLIAM BENNETT, travel writer

Percentage of parents who own RVs and consider them the best way to travel with children

Jet lag is a temporary disruption of bodily rhythms caused by high-speed travel across several time zones typically in a jet aircraft. It affects 94% of long-haul flyers and includes such physical symptoms as fatigue, insomnia, disorientation, swelling limbs, ear/nose/eye irritations, headaches, bowel irregularity and light-headedness. Jet lag occurs because changes in time zones confuse the body's 24-hour inner clock known as 'circadian rhythms'.

• Avoid caffeine and alcohol.

• Isocones (pushing acupressure points) help you sleep during the journey.

• Travel west is best: arrive in the late afternoon if possible because then you don't have to wait long till bedtime and will be fresh the following morning.

• If travelling east arrive in the morning – and try to get straight into the sunlight as the body clock takes its timing from natural sunlight and will adjust eastwards more quickly.

• Adapt to your new time zone as quickly as possible, especially at meal and sleep times.

• Change your watch to your destination time zone on the plane. Sleep on the plane if it is bedtime in your arrival city; stay awake if it isn't.

• One authority, which thinks that dehydration is the main culprit of jet lag, recommends that you drink two glasses of water before getting on the plane and one or more litres in flight.

• One German study found sedentary passengers suffered more jet lag than those who walked or exercised. Exercise, both in the air and upon arrival, will circulate your blood and help you feel rejuvenated.

• Adjust your sleep time before you leave on your trip. If you are flying from the west coast to the east coast of America, for example; if your normal bedtime is midnight, then three nights before you travel go to sleep at 11pm. Two days before you travel, retire at 10pm, and the night before your trip, go to sleep at 9pm. (which is midnight on the east coast).

• Take melatonin, an over-the counter product, which is being touted as the new miracle 'jet-lag pill'. It is a substance naturally produced in humans at night. Supposedly it tricks the body into resetting the natural sleep/awake cycle. If taken in the morning, it delays your body clock and allows you to stay up later. If taken at night, it encourages sleep.

PACK IT IN

When travelling, it's not always possible to lug around your worldly goods so a day-pack is a must-have. But what to put in? Here is a list of essential items for a 21st-century day-pack:

- passport
- water bottle
- small, light, folding waterproof
- a power bar for emergency rations
- a local language book with which to entertain guides
- small amount of cash
- spare photographic film
- a large handkerchief
- a plastic bag (multi-purpose: to sit on, fill with rubbish, put wet things in)

- plasters
- dark glasses
- camera
- note book for astonishing journal entries
- a clip of safety pins (multi-purpose: from laundry to gifts)
- small folding knife
- sarong or pashmina for cover up situations
- sun hat

Any more than this and it can no longer be termed a day-pack!

JOY RIDES

To become a member of the notorious Mile High Club, you need to engage in sexual intercourse while in an aeroplane, at least a mile above the earth's surface. Most people, although unsure of their exact altitude will claim to be members of this club having taken part in some kind of hanky-panky in a plane's lavatory.

This high altitude high-risk hobby can perhaps be traced back to a daring pilot in 1916. Lawrence Sperry grew up handsome and rich and his wild lifestyle earned him a regular place in the tabloids of the time. In November 1916 he began to give flying lessons to a New York socialite called Mrs Waldo Polk, whose husband was conveniently away driving an ambulance in France at the time. The pair became involved in some airborne antics, thanks to the newly devised autopilot. Unfortunately something went wrong with the plane and it plunged 500ft into the bay below. Rescuers were amazed to find that the couple had survived, albeit without clothing. Sperry claimed that the crash had divested them of their clothing but later confessed to causing the crash by knocking the gyro during a romantic encounter.

The tabloids, true to form, recognised a catchy headline a mile off and the *New York Mirror* and *Evening Graphic* ran with 'Aerial Petting Ends in Wetting'. They don't write 'em like they used to.

Now, in the Assir, I was standing on a mountain-side forested with wild olives and junipers. A stream tumbled down the slope; its water, ice-cold at 9,000 feet, was in welcome contrast with the scanty, bitter water of the sands. There were wild flowers: jasmine and honeysuckle, wild roses, pinks and primulas. There were terraced fields of wheat and barley, vines, and plots of vegetables. Far below me a yellow haze hid the desert to the east. Yet it was there that my fancies ranged, planning new journeys while I wondered at this strange compulsion, which drove me back to a life that was barely possible. It would, I felt, have been understandable if I had been working in some London office, dreaming of freedom and adventure; but here, surely, I had all that I could possibly desire on much easier terms. But I knew instinctively that it was the very hardness of life in the desert which drew me back there – it was the same pull which takes men back to the polar ice, to high mountains, and to the sea,

Wilfred Thesiger, *Arabian Sands*

TEN MOST POPULAR SOUVENIRS, NOT SO POPULAR WITH CITES' ENDANGERED SPECIES CONVENTION

1. Crocodile skin products from Thailand and the USA
2. Rock python skin products from Africa
3. Coral from South-east Asia and the Caribbean
4. Conch shells and clams from the Caribbean
5. Ivory and other elephant products from Africa and Asia
6. Hippo teeth from Africa and Asia
7. Turtle shell products from Sri Lanka, UAE and the Caribbean
8. Furs and skins from the big cats of South America and Africa
9. Parrots and toucans from China, Hong Kong and Thailand
10. Water monitor lizard's skin products from Asia and Nigeria

CITES (Convention on International Trade on Endangered Species) The 'Washington' Convention on International Trade in Endangered Species of Wild Fauna and Flora was launched in 1975 to protect endangered plants and animals. By controlling and overseeing their international trade, CITES seeks to prevent it reaching irreversible levels. More than 150 parties ratified the Convention, regulating international trade in over 30,000 species. CITES is administered by the United Nations Environment Programme (UNEP).

Percentage of Britons who said that using the Euro was easy when travelling 97 in Europe in 2003, the summer after it was introduced

-OLOGISTS WHO MAY WANT TO TRAVEL

Anthropologist
Study and analysis of the origins and characteristics of human beings and their societies, customs and beliefs.

Archaeologist
Excavation and subsequent study of the physical remains of earlier civilisations, especially buildings and artefacts, which now benefits from advances in scientific techniques such as carbon dating.

Deltiologist
Study and collection of picture postcards.

Dialectologist
Study of dialect.

Egyptologist
Study of the language, culture and history of ancient Egypt.

Ethnologist
Scientific study of different races and cultural traditions, and their relations with each other.

Sinologist
Study of China in all its aspects, especially cultural and political.

DISTINCTIVE DWELLINGS

Train carriages, Tennessee, USA and York, England
All aboard for the land of Nod! The USA is king when it comes to wacky hotels, and the Chattanooga Choo-Choo is no exception. Stay in the opulent surroundings of a Victorian train and eat in the elegant dining car.

The Sidings Hotel in Yorkshire is a more intimate affair. Four carriages have been divided into two restaurants, a comfy lounge and eight bedrooms. You won't get very far, but your stay will certainly be more pleasant – and possibly cheaper – than the average train journey these days.

THEY MUST LOVE US

Annual visits to the UK by overseas residents

1994	20.7 million
1995	23.5 million
1996	25.1 million
1997	25.5 million
1998	25.7 million
1999	25.3 million
2000	25.2 million
2001	22.8 million
2002	24.1 million

98 *The amount, in millions of dollars, British travellers spent while visiting their friends and relatives in North America during spring 2003*

Wiesbaden – the home of Captain Hook

14 FEARS TO KEEP YOU AT HOME

Aerophobia	air, flying
Gephyrophobia	crossing a bridge
Dromophobia	crossing streets
Demophobia	crowds
Hypsophobia	high places
Acrophobia, altophobia	heights
Kinesophobia, kinetophobia	motion
Agoraphobia	open spaces
Topophobia	places
Xenophobia	strangers, foreigners
Hodophobia	travel
Siderodromophobia	travelling by train
Amaxophobia	vehicles
Basiphobia	walking

Glancing back, they saw a small cloud of dust, with a dark centre of energy, advancing on them at incredible speed, while from out the dust a faint 'Poop-poop!' wailed like an uneasy animal in pain. Hardly regarding it, they turned to resume their conversation, when in an instant (as it seemed) the peaceful scene was changed, and with a blast of wind and a whirl of sound that made them jump for the nearest ditch, It was on them! the 'poop-poop' rang with a brazen shout in their ears, they had a moment's glimpse of an interior of glittering plate-glass and rich morocco, and the magnificent motor-car, immense, breath-snatching, passionate, with its pilot tense and hugging his wheel, possessed all earth and air for the fraction of a second, flung an enveloping cloud of dust that blinded and enwrapped them utterly, and then dwindled to a speck in the far distance, changed back into a droning bee once more.

The old grey horse, dreaming, as he plodded along, of his quiet paddock, in a new raw situation such as this simply abandoned himself to his natural emotions. Rearing, plunging, backing steadily, in spite of all the Mole's efforts at his head, and all the Mole's lively language directed at his better feelings, he drove the cart backwards towards the deep ditch at the side of the road. It wavered an instant – then there was a heartrending crash – and the canary-coloured cart, their pride and their joy, lay on its side in the ditch, an irredeemable wreck...

...The Rat came to help him [Mole], but their united efforts were not sufficient to right the cart. 'Hi! Toad!' they cried. 'Come and bear a hand, can't you!'

The Toad never answered a word, or budged from his seat in the road; so they went to see what was the matter with him. They found him in a sort of trance, a happy smile on his face, his eyes still fixed on the dusty wake of their destroyer. At intervals he was still heard to murmur 'Poop-poop!'

The Rat shook him by the shoulder. 'Are you coming to help us, Toad?' he demanded sternly.

'Glorious, stirring sight!' murmured Toad, never offering to move. 'The poetry of motion! The real way to travel! The only way to travel! Here to-day – in next week to-morrow! Villages skipped, towns and cities jumped – always somebody else's horizon! O bliss! O poop-poop! O my! O my!'

Kenneth Grahame, *The Wind in the Willows*

QUOTE UNQUOTE

An agreeable companion on a journey is as good as a carriage.
PUBLIUS SYRUS, Roman writer

TRAVELLERS' CHECKLISTS

To make sure you are well prepared and have a safe holiday, the 10 most important things to do according to the Foreign and Commonwealth Office are:

Check the Foreign and Commonwealth Office (FCO) travel advice on www.fco.gov.uk or call 0870 606 0290.

Get travel insurance and check that the cover is appropriate and for your whole trip, whether its one day or over a year. Make sure it covers you for all activities, including hazardous sports. Take your policy number and the 24-hour emergency number with you.

Get a good guidebook and get to know your destination. Find out about local laws and customs, especially relating to alcohol and drugs.

Ensure you have a valid passport and necessary visas. Also take another form of ID with you, preferably one with a photo.

Check what vaccinations you need at least six weeks before you go. Check if your medication is legal in the country you are visiting and take a letter from your GP and your prescription.

Check to see if you need to take extra health precautions, for example malaria cover.

Make sure your travel agent is an ABTA member and, if flying, make sure your holiday package is ATOL protected. If your travel involves passage on airlines with which you are unfamiliar, you may wish to check their safety and reliability with a reputable travel agent.

Make copies of your passport, insurance policy plus 24-hour emergency number, and ticket details – leave copies with family and friends.

Take enough money for your trip and some back-up funds eg travellers cheques, sterling or US dollars.

Leave a copy of your itinerary and a way of contacting you such as email, with family and friends.

BUSK OR BUST

A full time busker from North Wales decided in 2004 to take his music to a wider audience by busking around the world. Nigel Ashcroft will only travel using the earnings from his busking. The 29-year-old is planning on taking in Moscow, Barcelona, Hong Kong, Tokyo, Berlin, New York and Bangkok and delivering to them his repertoire of guitar-based performances.

FANTASTIC FESTIVITIES

Wife Carrying Championships
Sonkajärvi, Finland, *July*
Contestants must carry a wife (not necessarily theirs) round a 253.5m course of sand, grass, asphalt and water obstacles: 15 points deducted for a dropped wife, the wife's weight in beer for the winner.

International Regatta of Bathtubs
Dinant, Belgium, *August*
The fundamental rule of this (fundamental) nautical festival is... yes, bathtubs. No motors are allowed, and the influence of local businesses goes further than sponsoring the event – meat cleavers and other implements are used to paddle the rafts. Contestants may douse each other with buckets of water, however, rules forbid the deliberate sinking of competitors.

BATTLE OF THE BEACH

The culturally rich and interesting rivalry we have with our old friends the Germans is not something left behind when we head off on holiday, for it is precisely at these times that our paths seem to cross.

And let's face it, the tardy Brit who optimistically wonders down to the water expecting to find a really nice spot only to find rows of German holiday-makers laid out like cards in a game of pairs needs a little help. Now a holiday company has devised a towel territory rating table, covering all of Europe's top beaches, assessing each on its towel-to-person ratio. Measured by taking the size of a beach, dividing this by the size of the average towel, and then again by the average number of visitors, it's calculated

that San Antonio on Ibiza is the English man's hardest target, with 1.1 towels per person. The Isla Canela, on the other hand, tucked away on the Costa de la Luz in southern Spain, has a whopping 14.5 towels per person, giving us a far higher chance of success.

Choosing a beach and marking your territory is only half the battle, though. Suggested tactics thereafter include: putting the children to work building sandcastles, apparently no one likes to trample such creations; putting up wind shields, however windy; using an inflatable; starting a game of bat and ball (don't hold back on the swing); and finding the danger element in any 'game' and using it to your advantage.

ONE HUMP NOT TWO

Camel facts for the one humped dromedary

• Camels can travel two weeks with no food or water.

• They can walk for 18 hours a day covering 20–25 miles.

• Pushed to limits camels can travel over 100 miles a day.

• They have two toes which splay out to form a huge surface area to stop them sinking in the sand.

• Before a long journey camels are made to drink and store large quantities of water in their stomachs.

• After a long journey a camel can drink up to 30 gallons/136 litres/240 pints water at a single sitting.

• Fatty deposits in their humps are metabolised to provide nutrients and water during lean periods.

• They can lose a third of their body weight without harm.

• Although humans become ill if their body temp rises more than 3.3°C (6°F) camels don't even sweat until their body temperature has raised 9°C (16°F) above the norm.

• Dromedaries have been domesticated for 3,000 years – there's no such thing as a truly feral camel now.

• The two-humped bactrian camel of central and eastern Asia with its thick coat can survive the bitter winter temperatures of the Gobi desert.

SHARK ATTACK!

	Fatal Attacks	Total Attacks
1. USA	69	855
2. Australia	152	323
3. South Africa	43	225
4. Hawaii	19	99
5. Brazil	20	78
6. Papua New Guinea	31	65
7. New Zealand	9	53
8. The Bahamas	1	42
9. Mexico	21	39
10. Fiji Islands	10	25

A total of 2,000 attacks have been recorded since the 16th century by The International Shark Attack File. With 536 attacks, the 1990s saw the highest attack total, reflecting the rising popularity in aquatic activities.

LEFT OR RIGHT?

Curiously the Swedes, like all their neighbours, drove on the right until 1736 when they decided to drive on the left. In 1967, they decided to change back again, so, in an ordered Scandinavian way, at 5am on Sunday 3 September they reverted back to the right-hand side of the road. They stopped public transport for up to 24 hours so as not to confuse the issue. Soldiers were called out to alter traffic lights and turn signs around. The national speed limit was drastically reduced and raised in small steps over the following months until it was back to normal and everyone had got used to driving on the right/wrong/right side of the road.

TRAVEL NOTES

Kusma, a large Hindu village near the Kali Gandaki River, lies at about 3,000 feet, nearly the lowest point of altitude on this journey. Phu-Tsering replenishes our supplies with fresh cucumbers and guavas, and by noon we are under way once more, moving north along the eastern bank. In the first village on the river is a small wood temple, with two stone cows decked out in red hibiscus; on a stone head in the temple wall is another unfathomable smile. The village creaks to the soft rhythm of an ancient treadle, and under the windows babies sway in their wicker baskets. In the serene and indiscriminate domesticity of these sunny villages, sow and piglet, cow and calf, mother and infant, hen and chicks, nanny and kid commingle in a common pulse of being. We eat papaya at the tea house, and afterwards bathe in the deep pools of a mountain torrent that comes foaming down over pale rocks beyond the village. On this last day of September I linger for a while in a warm waterfall, in the moist sun, while my washed clothes bake dry upon the stones.

All afternoon the trail continues up the Kali Gandaki, which rushes down from Mustang and Tibet onto the Ganges plain; because it flows between the soaring massifs of Annapurna and Dhaulagiri, both more than 26,000 feet in altitude, the Kali Gandaki has the deepest canyon of any river in the world. Kali signifies 'black female' or 'dark woman', and it is true that its steep walls, grey torrent, and black boulders give a hellish darkness to this river. Fierce Kali the Black, the female aspect of Time and Death, and the Devourer of All Things, is the consort of the Hindu god of the Himalaya, Great Shiva the Re-Creator and Destroyer; her black image, with its necklace of human skulls, is the emblem of this dark river that, rumbling down out of hidden peaks and vast clouds of unknowing, has filled the traveller with dread since the first human tried to cross and was borne away.

A far cicada rings high and clear over the river's heavy wash.

Peter Matthiessen, *The Snow Leopard*

HOW GREEN IS MY VIKING?

After three years of exile spent exploring the coast of Greenland, Erik the Red returned to Iceland in 986. To entice Icelandic inhabitants to settle on the huge icy island he had recently discovered, he somewhat distorted the truth and named it Greenland! It worked.

According to the Sagas of Greenland, his son, Leif Eriksson, a noble and sophisticated 'Golden' Viking, ventured even further west and was the first European to try to colonise the far North-east coast of the American continent. He landed on the shores of present day Newfoundland, and called it Vinland, or Wine Land, because of the red berries found there. However, the original colony of 35 did not remain there for long. By the end of the 15th century, the settlements of the Norse peoples in Greenland had withered away. Perhaps disease, the local people or a mini ice age may have driven them away.

The Vikings were great sea travellers, mastering the seas and the coasts of the northern Atlantic world. The memories of their adventures were kept alive by their tradition of oral storytelling so that when Columbus's brother Bartholomew visited Bristol, which was the largest fishing port in the North Atlantic at the time, he might have heard of tales of 'the foggy lands of the West'.

TRAVEL TEASERS

A train enters a tunnel at seven o'clock, another train enters the exact same tunnel, also at seven o'clock on the same day. The tunnel only has one track, and no other means for the trains to pass, around, over, or under. However, both trains made it to the other end of the tunnel untouched. How could this be?

Answer on page 153

COME SEE THE KHAMSEEN

Khamseen means 50; so called because this hot south-westerly Egyptian wind, coming from the Sahara, blows for about 50 days from April until June. The term was coined by the early Arabic speaking Christians to designate the period of days following Easter which lead to the feast of Pentecost, a Greek word meaning the 50th day. Khamseen is not originally the name of the storm but of the season during which these dusty winds are particularly abundant.

The same wind in the Sudan is known as Haboob. In Morocco it is called Chergui, Harmattan in Algeria, Chehili in Tunisia, Ghibli in Lybia – and for most westerners, it is simply the Sirocco.

USEFUL TIPS FOR TREKKERS

Fill your water bottle at night with hot tea. Put it in a sock. Put that down your sleeping bag and you have: a hot water bottle; warm, dry socks; and tea in which to brush your teeth in the morning.

Purified water's not that tasty: an effervescent vitamin tablet in your drinking water takes the bad taste away.

If you wash your knickers and socks but don't have time to dry them, pin them on your day-pack and they'll dry in the sun by lunch. Remember to pack lots of nappy pins, which not only make good roadside presents, but come in handy in many unexpected ways – for instance pinning drying laundry to your pack.

Large square handkerchiefs are multi-purpose: not only useful for blowing the lining of your nose into at high altitude, you can also protect the back of your neck from the sun, and wrap them round your face in dust storms.

A book of short stories is better than one long tale. You can read one out to your travelling companions after dinner before you all pass out with exhaustion.

Energy tablets are very boring, repetitive, and so high in citric acid that in large doses they give you as bad an upset stomach as some trekking food. Pack tasty alternatives such as dried fruit or Biltong, strips of meat that are salted and dried in the sun.

Trekking food can be very plain: take with you things to spice up the offered fare – marmite and brown sauce (in unbreakable plastic containers) can make all the difference to a tasteless steamed vegetable dumpling.

FOOD FJORDS

The Norwegians are a hospitable people. Along the ancient trails and trekking routes through their forests are many comfortably appointed huts in which the passing traveller is welcome to stay the night – on the understanding that they leave the hut tidy and as well equipped as it was when they arrived. So, for instance, if you arrive to find there's coffee, ham and cheese, you're welcome to these as long as you replace them before you leave.

QUOTE UNQUOTE

Travel is fatal to prejudice, bigotry, and narrow-mindedness, and many of our people need it sorely on these accounts.
MARK TWAIN, writer

TRAVEL NOTES

There it lay at last, the bourn of my long and weary pilgrimage, realising the plans and hopes of many and many a year. The mirage medium of Fancy invested the huge catafalque and its gloomy pall with peculiar charms. There were no giant fragments of hoar antiquity as in Egypt, no remains of graceful and harmonious beauty as in Greece and Italy; yet the view was strange, unique – and how few have looked upon the celebrated shrine! I may truly say that, of all the worshippers who clung weeping to the curtain, or who pressed their beating hearts to the stone, none felt for the moment a deeper emotion than did the Hajji from the far-north. It was as if the poetical legends of the Arab spoke truth, and that the wavering wings of angels, not the sweet breeze of morning, were agitating and swelling the black covering of the shrine. But, to confess humbling truth, theirs was the high feeling of religious enthusiasm, mine was the ecstasy of gratified pride.

Richard Burton, on his arrival at Mecca in 1853
His intention was to be the 'first unconverted Englishman to visit Mecca of his own free will, posing as a true Mohammedan pilgrim'.

OUTSTANDING AIRPORTS

King Khalid International Airport in Riyadh, Saudi Arabia is the largest airport in the world at 87 square miles. By comparison, London Heathrow is 4.7 square miles.

Atlanta's Hartsfield Jackson airport is the busiest in terms of passengers, handling close to 80 million passengers a year, but London Heathrow is the busiest in terms of international passengers (many American flights are domestic).

London is the busiest city in aviation terms – with Heathrow, Gatwick, Stansted, Luton and London City combined, it handles a total of almost 120 million passengers annually.

TRAVEL TIPS

When presented with a landing card, or visa application think hard before you claim to practice an unusual profession. It's not always a good idea to say you're self-employed. Countries are nervous of people who might end up costing them money. So it can be worth calling yourself a secretary when you are in fact a journalist or a photographer.

'THE REAL WAY TO TRAVEL!
THE ONLY WAY TO TRAVEL!'

Toad, from *The Wind in the Willows*, was just one of many for whom the advent of the motor car stimulated dreams of great travel...

By the early 20th century, there were over 8,000 motor vehicles in the US alone. In August 1907, Prince Borghese of Italy won the 8,000-mile Peking to Paris motor race in 62 days, overcoming problems from a bush fire to a Belgian policeman who booked him for speeding, in order to win his prize.

In 1908, the French paper *Le Matin* staged the first around the world car race. It was won by an American Thomas vehicle which took 170 days to cover the 13,500-mile course. The six car competition took place in an era when paved highways were almost unknown: there were no road maps, tires were fragile and cars frail. Six cars and a score of men competed. The only American car to compete was the winning Thomas Flyer.

Steep gradients were apparently no problem to the early motorist – in 1911, the first driver topped Ben Nevis, Britain's highest peak at 4,406ft.

Ian Fleming's fantasmagorical *Chitty Chitty Bang Bang* was inspired by a car built in 1920 by a certain Count Zborowski on his estate near Canterbury. His car's vast engine was encased in a grey steel body with a polished hood eight feet long. She weighed over five tonnes – in spite of which she managed to win the 1921 Brooklands 100mph short handicap at 101 miles per hour.

In 1957, teams from Oxford and Cambridge raced Landrovers overland from Paris to Singapore negotiating particularly tough ground in Eastern India, and taking some of the war built Stillwell road through Burma. Oxford won.

The Paris–Dakar Rally pits over 400 drivers against one another in a gruelling 17-day race over 6,500 miles. Competitors race all sorts of off road vehicles over the toughest terrain and conditions. The Paris–Dakar originated in 1978, a year after Thierry Sabine got lost in the desert and decided it might be a good place for a rally.

There is another rally to Dakar, starting from Plymouth – but the competitors in this race are not allowed to spend more than £100 on their vehicles and no more than £15 on special race preparations. Most of the vehicles are held together with duct tape and none, so far, have reached Dakar.

As she felt its gentle twang for the 17th time, Carmen wondered what Carlos' over-familiar guitar would look like wrapped round his fat grinning face.

CALM BEFORE THE STORM

The Pacific Ocean is known for some of the most powerful storms in the world, producing swells in excess of 100ft high. The first westerner to sail its treacherous waters in 1519, Ferdinand Magellan had the remarkable luck to cross it without encountering any storms at all! So he misnamed it Mar Pacifico (the calm sea). Magellan was killed fighting for a friendly native king in the Philippines in 1521 but one of his ships, under the captainship of a certain Juan Sebastian del Cano, made it back to Spain, so completing the first circumnavigation of the globe in 1522.

TRAVEL TEASERS

A car's odometer shows 72,927 miles, a palindromic number. What are the minimum miles you would need to travel to form another?
Answer on page 153

AIR WAYS

All airports are abbreviated to a three letter code: just so you know where you are...

JFK	John F Kennedy – New York
JKT	Jakarta – Indonesia
LHR	London – Heathrow
LGW	London – Gatwick
LCY	London – City airport
LPL	John Lennon – Liverpool
BQH	Biggin Hill – UK
SFO	San Francisco – USA
MOW	Sheremetyevo 2 – Moscow
THR	Teheran
WOL	Wollogong – Australia
ZAG	Zagreb
LAX	Los Angeles

WELCOME ABOARD

The first ever air hostess was called Ellen Church and was employed by Boeing Air Transport. She was no trolley dolly though: she was hired for her nursing skills rather than her ability to serve customers. She applied to be a pilot, but the traffic manager of BAT was more keen on hiring her as a nurse to calm passengers as although air travel was becoming more common, most thought it too dangerous to even try.

Ellen became a stewardess on 15 May 1930 and worked the route between Oakland and Chicago. Stewardessing soon took off (pun intended) and many airlines boasted inflight service.

The requirements were very strict: a stewardess had to be a registered nurse; single; under 25; weigh less than 8 stone 2oz; and be less than 5ft 4in. This was largely motivated by the small size of early aircrafts which had narrow aisles, low ceilings and could not carry extra weight. The stewardesses were required to haul luggage, fuel planes and help pilots push planes into hangars as well as serve the passengers with sandwiches and coffee.

What is it about Cuba that draws so many...?

Ernest Hemingway's *The Old Man and the Sea* opens in Havana.

In 1946, mobster Lucky Luciano called a summit in Havana. The meeting was held at the Hotel Nacional, the hotel famously built with Mafia money. The meeting was attended by a who's who of mobsters – Meyer Lansky, Frank Costello, Tommy Lucchese, Vito Genovese, Joe Bonanno, Santo Trafficante Jr and Moe Dalitz. Among the topics for discussion was the assassination of gangster Bugsy Siegel.

In 1946, Frank Sinatra made his singing debut in Havana.

On 10 December 1959, the Hotel Riviera opened in Havana. It cost US$14 million to build and most of the money was supplied by the Cuban government (the old Batista regime – Castro hadn't quite seized power yet) to the owner Meyer Lansky. The floor-show in the Copa Room was headlined that night by Ginger Rogers. Lansky wasn't impressed: he was heard to say that Rogers 'can wiggle her ass, but she can't sing a goddamn note.'

Guantanamo Bay was originally a holiday resort, and was leased to the US Navy in 1898. The terms of the lease require Washington to pay rent which was set a century ago at 2,000 gold coins a year, rent which is now worth a very good value US$4,000. The lease can only be voided by mutual agreement or abandonment of the land by the US.

The Buena Vista Social Club, that lovely lazy sounding salsa band, comes from Santiago in Cuba, a place where music surrounds you all day. Even the lift attendant in the Ambos Mundos hotel (where Hemingway used to stay) in Havana will dance with you if there's a gap in the need for the lift.

TRAVEL NOTES

A blustering storm was rushing and whistling between the wheels of the train and round the pillars and the corners of the station. The railway carriages, the pillars, the people, and everything that could be seen, were covered on one side with snow, and that covering became thicker and thicker. A momentary lull would be followed by such a terrific gust that it seemed hardly possible to stand against it. Yet people, merrily exchanging remarks, ran over the creaking boards of the platform, and the big station doors were constantly being opened and shut.

Tolstoy, *Anna Karenina*

TRAVELLING WITH A CONSCIENCE

Travelling is part of modern life but the consequences on the environment can be huge. Here are some of the negative effects of travelling, and what you can do to reverse the trend:

42% of a hotel's energy use is used on heating water, yet the majority of guests are willing to use their sheets and towels for more than one day. Use hotels that use a 'no change' policy or write your own note to the chambermaid.

When on holiday, much of the money tourists spend does not go to the local people but to large tour operators, hotels and on imported food and drink. For every £100 spent on a holiday in a developing country, only around £5 actually stays in the country's economy. With so many developing countries relying on tourism for income, try and spend locally on hotels, goods and food.

Water is a big issue in travelling. When abroad, the average tourist can use over 800 litres of water in 24 hours. Try and conserve water while you are travelling and encourage your hotel to introduce water saving techniques.

Aviation produces more carbon dioxide than all human activity in Africa. And one long-haul return flight can produce more CO_2 per passenger than the average motorist produces in a year. This means that by 2015, over half the annual destruction of the ozone layer could be caused by air travel. One way to offset this trend is to pay voluntary tax at airports, for example at Luton where the money goes towards planting a tree around the town to help soak up the carbon emissions from the planes.

QUOTE UNQUOTE

The trouble about journeys nowadays is that they are easy to make but difficult to justify. The earth, which once danced and spun before us alluringly as a celluloid ball on top of a fountain in a rifle-range, is now a dull and vulnerable target.
PETER FLEMING, travel writer

TRAVEL TIPS

Make sure you take a large bottle of water with you when flying since air travel is one of the most dehydrating activities known to man. You should drink approximately 120 millilitres every hour and avoid alcohol, as it will only dehydrate you further. Applying moisturiser can also help prevent dry skin.

SOME TRAVELLERS FROM YESTERYEAR

1. Marco Polo (1254–1324)
A Venetian merchant and adventurer, Marco Polo spent more than 20 years journeying from Europe to China, and his accounts have become classic travel literature.

2. Christopher Columbus (1451–1506)
Of Genoese origin, it was under the King and Queen of Spain's patronage that he arrived in the Caribbean instead of India, being one of the first Europeans to 'discover' the Americas.

3. Vasco de Gama (1460–1524)
A Portuguese navigator famous for opening up a new sea route from Europe to Asia via the Cape of Good Hope in Southern Africa, an expedition that boosted Portugal to become a world power.

3. Ferdinand Magellan (1480–1521)
Magellan, a Portuguese navigator and explorer, was the first person to circumnavigate the globe. He started from Spain, reached South America, and crossed the Pacific via the Magellan Strait, as it's now known, to the Philippines.

5. Sir Francis Drake (1540-1596)
It took Drake, an English navigator, three years to successfully complete Magellan's voyage, arriving home in a ship brimming with exotic spices and treasures.

ALL CHANGE!

Borders where you have to pull over and drive on the opposite side of the road:

The bridge over the Mekong: You drive on the left in Thailand; the right in Laos.

The right in China; at the border with Pakistan, there's a sign saying: 'Entering Pakistan. Drive on left'.

The left in Hong Kong; the right in China

The left in Namibia; the right in Angola

The right in Zaire; the left in Uganda

FANTASTIC FESTIVITIES

Tunarama, Port Lincoln, South Australia, *January*
This fish festival originated to celebrate the town's fish industry, which is centred on the tuna. The highlight of the annual January festival is the world championship tuna-tossing event where the city turns out to watch hearty men and women try and hurl the fish as far as possible.

KNOT MANY PEOPLE KNOW THIS

In times gone by, a captain would calculate his ship's speed by throwing a wooden log into the water and observing how fast it moved away from the ship. This approximate method of ship speed measurement was called 'Heaving the Log' and was used until the mid-1600s when the 'Chip Log' method was invented, probably by Dutch sailors.

The 'Chip Log' apparatus consisted of a small, weighted wood panel that was attached to a reel of rope and a half-minute sand glass. The rope had knots tied at equal distances along its length. Sailors would throw the wood panel into the sea and the rope would start unwinding from the reel. The faster the ship was moving the faster the rope would unwind. By counting the number of knots that went overboard in a given time, they could calculate the ship's speed. And that is the origin of the nautical speed unit: the knot.

So, how fast is a knot? It is equivalent to the nautical mile, which is 1.15 miles/hr or 1.85km/hr.

TRAVEL NOTES

April 17th

Well, Dorothy and I are really at London. I mean we got to London on the train yesterday as the boat does not come clear up to London but it stops on the beach and you have to take a train. I mean everything is much better in New York, because the boat comes right up to New York and I am really beginning to think that London is not so educational after all. But I did not tell Mr Eisman when I cabled him last night because Mr Eisman really sent me to London to get educated and I would hate to tell him that London is a failure because we know more in New York.

So Dorothy and I came to the Ritz and it is delightfully full of Americans. I mean you would really think it was New York because I always think that the most delightful thing about travelling is to always be running into Americans and to always feel at home.

Anita Loos, *Gentlemen Prefer Blondes*

QUOTE UNQUOTE

The great and recurrent question about abroad is,
is it worth getting there?
Attributed to ROSE MACAULAY, novelist

MIRACULOUS SURVIVOR

On 8 October 1568, Job Horton was set on land somewhere in the Bay of Mexico where he was taken prisoner by the Spanish. He recorded the next 23 years of his life as follows:

> I suffered imprisonment in Mexico, two years.
> In the Contractation House in Seville, one year.
> In the Inquisition House in Triana, one year.
> I was in the galleys, twelve years.
> In the everlasting prison remediless, with the coat with St Andrew's cross on my back, four years.
> And at liberty I served as a drudge Hernando de Soria three years, which is the full complement of 23 years.
> Since my departure from England until this time of my return I was five times in great danger of death, besides the many perils I was in in the galleys.
> First, in the port of St John de Ulua, where being on shore with many other of our company, which were all slain saving I and two other that by swimming got aboard the Jesus of Lubeck.
> Secondly, when we were robbed by the wild Indians.
> Thirdly after we came to Mexico, the Viceroy would have hanged us.
> Fourthly, because he could not have his mind to hang us he would have burnt us.
> Fifthly, the General that brought us into Spain would have hanged us at sea.

> Thus, having truly set down unto you my travails, misery and dangers, endured the space of 23 years, I end.

NO PLACE LIKE NOME?

The town of Nome in Alaska is so called because an Alaskan-British map dated 1850 was misread – what the map actually said was 'Name?' Nome had its heyday during the Gold Rush of 1898, which brought 20,000 people to the area when it was found that even the sand on the beach had gold scattered in it. A railway was built to Nome in 1900 and the town is still there, in spite of a fire in 1934 which destroyed most of the buildings from the Gold Rush era. Now Nome's known as a start-out point for visiting Alaska's glorious wilderness – on which the miners' shovels and panning equipment can still be found.

Nome has also been commemorated in a Pixar animation short film entitled *Knick Knack* (1989) which stars a snowman in a snowglobe labelled Nome, Alaska. The film appears on the DVD of *Finding Nemo* (2003), a film about a little fish whose name, oddly, is an anagram of Nome.

GUIDE TO APPROPRIATE TRAVEL CLOTHING

1. DESERT
Where
Africa: Sahara, Kalahari;
Australia: Simpson;
Oman: Empty Quarter

Protection from the sun

What
• Long-sleeved cotton shirts and trousers, some of which now have sun protection factors.
• Sunscreens, neckerchiefs, wide-brimmed hats, sunglasses, sometimes even goggles, suede or fabric 'desert shoes', with thick soles and breathability, fibre-pile jacket, warm hat for cold nights.

2. TROPICAL
Where
Malaysia, Amazonia, Indonesia, Congo, Madagascar

Protection from leeches and rain

What
• Jungle boots or canvas baseball boots, with leech-proof vents where water can drain; spare pair needed if journey lasts more than a few months.
• Loose, light cotton clothing, not military patterned!, poncho, soft hat and bandana to keep sweat and leeches off your face; keep spare dry set in sealed waterproof bag.
• Knee-length socks, tightly woven and strong seams to prevent leeches from coming in, insect repellent and a leech-stick (a piece of wood with salt),

some clothing is already impregnated with it.

3. MOUNTAIN
Where
Himalayas, Alps, Andes, Alaska, New Zealand, Pamirs (Tajikistan), Karakoram (Pakistani Himalayas)

Protection from the cold

What
• Flexible layering system: fast-dry synthetic base, fleece for the mid-layer, waterproof and breathable shell
• No cotton, wide-hat, sunglasses, umbrella, fleece hat and gloves
• Boots, either leather or fabric, with ankle protection, thick tread and midsole

4. SOUTH POLE

Protection from freezing cold, your own sweat

What
• Synthetic long-johns, long-sleeved top, windproof fleece jacket, ventile sledging jacket (the first weatherproof/breath-able jacket), fibre-pile salopettes(breathable material), waterproof/breathable nylon overtrousers
• Inner gloves, waterproof, breathable outer mitts, thermal lightweight fleece mask, wind-proof headband, inner, vapour barrier and outer socks, plastic double boots, overgaiters.

NATURAL REMEDIES

All over the world western medicine is being given new ideas by the traditional medicines used by indigenous peoples:

Pineapples, used for medicinal purposes by the Guarani Indians of Brazil and Paraguay, contain an enzyme which could prevent thrombosis.

The cancer-curing potential of the rosy periwinkle was brought to the attention of western scientists by the traditional healers of Jamaica and Madagascar.

In Sarawak, Borneo, people use the 'tuba akar' plant to cure fever. The plant is also a useful fish poison.

Chinchona officinalis, first used by South American Indians to cure fevers is now a source of quinine for the treatment of malaria.

Australian Aborigines use the sap, leaves and bark of gum trees to control bleeding and to treat burns, wounds, cuts and bites.

The dragon tree of the Canary Islands can grow to great heights and live for thousands of years. It secretes a sap called dragon's blood which the locals, a people called the Guanches used to staunch the flow of blood. You can still see dragon trees: in near Icod, a village on Tenerife, stands an immense example, probably the oldest in the Canaries. It's less easy to find Guanches – as a people they were discovered when the Spanish first arrived on the Canary Islands. They lived a stone-age existence, sheltering in caves, dressing in goat skins and eating cheese and a kind of flour. They didn't know about metal but still managed to fight off the marauding Spaniards for nearly a century before, decimated by their enemies, plague and famine they died out.

Closer to home, willow bark is an ancient European remedy, the properties of which are the basis of Aspirin, one of the world's oldest recognised analgesics.

FANTASTIC FESTIVITIES

Reveillon, Rio de Janeiro, Brazil, *December*
Every December the people of Rio pay tribute to the goddess of the sea, Yemanja. General festivities of dancing and chanting lead up to the launching of tiny boats and baskets with offerings aboard.
Popular gifts for the goddess include perfume, combs, mirrors, fried fish and watermelon.

If the gifts are carried out to sea, the boat owner will see good luck, but if the waves wash the offerings back ashore, the worshippers' prayers will be ignored.

THE 10 MOST USEFUL LANGUAGES

Mandarin – 1,075 million speakers
English – 514 million speakers
Hindustani – 496 million speakers
Spanish – 425 million speakers
Russian – 275 million speakers
Arabic – 256 million speakers
Bengali – 215 million speakers
Portuguese – 194 million speakers
Malay/Indonesian – 176 million speakers
French – 129 million speakers

ONLY IN AMERICA...

Cadillac Graveyard

In Bushland, Texas there are several Cadillac cars sticking half way out of the ground. The story behind this strange sight is that a rich oil tycoon once bought a brand new Cadillac but unfortunately it went to Cadillac heaven a bit sooner than he had hoped. Said tycoon then proceeded to try and get his money back but was refused. Such was his disgust that he decided to make a point by buying a brand new Cadillac every year and bury it in the ground on his vast property. As you do.

The Paper House

Rockport in Massachusetts can boast a rolled newspaper house. Well done them. Elis Stenman took newspapers and rolled them. And then he used them to design the interior walls of his house and build furniture with. Over 20 years he stained and hardened huge amounts of newspaper to allow them to be used as furniture. From lamps, tables and chairs, Stenman even has a piano of paper.

Corn Palace

When your state boasts the impressive and much visited Mount Rushmore, how do you compete? Well the people of Mitchell, South Dakota are having a good go. They have taken the rather obvious choice of constructing a Corn Palace, a building structured like a castle, and every year since 1892 they staple different colours of corn cobs onto the building, creating pictures like Indians around a fire, or a horse and carriage. Ah, that old chestnut.

The tallest thermometer in the world

Ever had trouble reading the tiny scale on a regular sized thermometer and wondered if they could make it just a little bit bigger? Well they have and they didn't just make it a bit bigger. The world's tallest thermometer is based in Baker, California and stands at 134ft high, a reminder of the highest temperature ever recorded in the US at nearby Death Valley in 1934.

JOURNEY'S END

John Keats

John Keats died in Rome, of tuberculosis, in February 1821 aged 25. For the last few months of his life Keats lived in a room, the ceiling of which was painted with big white daisies on a blue background, in a dusty pink house, the Casina Rossa, at the foot of the Spanish Steps. His friend, the painter Joseph Severn, used to nip across the road to the Café Greco (still there) for 19th century style takeaways, which he'd heat up on the fire in Keats's room.

Keats is buried in Rome's Protestant Cemetery. You can visit the room where he died, though all the original furniture in it was burned after his death on Papal orders.

TRAVEL TIPS

Money

In third world countries, it's often difficult to buy the currency before you get there. When you do, ask for lots of small denomination notes since outside large cities things will be very cheap and locals won't take kindly to being asked to change large notes.

Being armed with lots of small notes makes tipping easy too. American Dollars: a fistful of these will be welcomed in an emergency almost anywhere in the world.

Buy a cheap wallet and put some local coins in it and keep it in your pocket, for the pickpockets. You will then have protected your real money and the pickpocket will be none the wiser until it is too late.

The cheap wallet will also give quick access to coins and small money you might need in a hurry without digging into your secret stash when in public.

TRAVEL NOTES

Now I had always supposed I had travelled very little, restricted as I am by my responsibilities in the house... as I motored on in the sunshine towards the Berkshire border, I continued to be surprised by the familiarity of the country around me.

But then eventually the surroundings grew unrecognisable and I knew I had gone beyond all previous boundaries. I have heard people describe the moment, when setting sail in a ship, when one finally loses sight of the land. I imagine that experience of unease mixed with exhilaration often described in connection with this moment is very similar to what I felt in the Ford as the surroundings grew strange around me.

Kazuo Ishiguro, *Remains of the Day*

'One small step for a man,' uttered William H Braindead on his maiden voyage, 'one giant leap for maaaaaaaaaaaaaaaaaah...'

TRAVEL TEASERS

What travels round the world but always remains in a corner?
Answer on page 153

120 *Distance, in feet, of the first ever flight by the Wright brothers, shorter than a modern Boeing 747's wingspan*

LEFT OR RIGHT?

Exceptions to the rules

In Canada, on Route 20, the Lachine rapids near Montreal: crossing bridges allow you to change back into the natural right hand flow at each end.

The Parnell Bridge in Cork, Ireland: you drive over on the right.

The Ponte Palatino and the Ponte Pietro Nenni in Rome, Italy: you drive over on the wrong side.

The Parc des les Cascades in Barcelona, Spain: you drive around on the left.

Savoy court, off the Strand, London, UK: you drive on the right. This is not only the main entrance to the hotel, but also to the theatre. The rule was instituted in 1929 so that cars queueing to drop people at the theatre wouldn't block access to the hotel.

Interstate 5 from the North into LA: you drive on the left.

When the Argentine invaded the Falkland Islands the islanders were forced to drive on the right. However, this situation was soon reversed.

DOCTOR WHO

The recommended traveller's first-aid box, according to the World Health Organisation, should include:

Adhesive tape	Antiseptic wound cleaner
Bandages	Emollient eye drops
Insect repellent	Insect bite treatment
Nasal decongestant	Oral re-hydration salts
Scissors and safety pins	Simple analgesic such as paracetamol
Sterile dressing	Clinical thermometer

CHANGING WITH THE TIMES

In 1895 the *Times of London* decided to produce a new atlas for Great Britain. Regarded as the best in the world at the time, German cartographers were given the job of drawing 118 maps. The atlas included a map of the solar system and the movements of planets and moons. Half the plates in this first edition concentrated on Europe. A second edition was needed to show the political changes after World War I. In this edition Europe only took up a third of the plates. In the atlas printed in 1955–1959, after World War II, Europe was given space in even less pages as European colonial power waned. *The Times Atlas* has been revised and updated and republished at regular intervals ever since.

Discrepancy, in number of leagues, between how far Columbus thinks 121
he's travelled that day and what he tells his crew on 1 October 1492

- Formed 60 million years ago
- 8,850m (29,035ft)
- Called Sagarmatha (goddess of the sky) in Nepali
- Called Chomolungma (mother goddess of the universe) in Tibetan
- Named after Sir George Everest in 1865, the British surveyor-general of India. Once known as Peak 15
- Mount Everest rises a few millimetres each year: the Himalayas are still growing
- Location: 27°59' N, Longitude 86°56' E. The summit ridge separates Nepal and Tibet
- First ascent: 29 May 1953 by Sir Edmund Hillary, New Zealand and Tenzing Norgay, Nepal, via the South Col route
- First solo ascent: 20 August 1980 by Reinhold Messner, Italy, via the North-east ridge to the North Face
- First winter ascent: 17 February 1980 by L Cichy and K Wielicki, Poland
- First oxygenless ascent: 8 May 1978 by Reinhold Messner, Italy and Peter Habeler, Austria, via south-east ridge
- First ski descent: 10 July 2000 by Davo Karnicar, Slovenia
- Corpses remaining on Everest: about 120
- Fastest descent: In 1988, Jean-Marc Boivin of France descended in 11 minutes – paragliding
- First British woman to summit: Rebecca Stevens (in 1993)

DISTINCTIVE DWELLINGS

Love Hotels, Japan

Many trips to Japan will result in accommodation with a difference. Visitors can stay in a traditional *ryokan*, or inn, where rooms are separated by sliding screen doors, tatami mats adorn the floors and guests sleep Japanese-style, on futons.

If claustrophobia isn't a problem for you, try a capsule hotel. Home of the travelling businessman on a budget, guests climb up into their own tubes, with barely enough room to sit up in bed.

For something really different try a Love Hotel. Love hotels offer privacy for couples usually forced to live in close proximity to the rest of their families, as well as for those looking for extra-marital antics. Rooms are available by the night or hour and check-in procedures are completed via a computer in the lobby. There is enough entertainment in the rooms to keep you amused if you don't just have love on the mind: rooms come with karaoke, remote-control audio-visual systems and, an adventure in themselves, electronic toilets. You can find Love Hotels in every town, usually on the outskirts.

TRAVEL TEASERS

Travelling to a city, you lose your way. You come to a fork in the road and don't know which road to take. Standing at the fork are two men. Next to the men is a sign, which you may assume is correct, which states that one of the two men always tells the truth and the other always tells lies (but it is not known which is which). The sign goes on to say that travellers can only ask one of the men one question. What question can you pose that will give you the information you need to choose the correct road?

Answer on page 153

ARE YOU SURE YOU WANT TO FLY?

Long periods of time spent sitting still in the cramped conditions of an airplane can cause deep vein thrombosis. To prevent this, invest in special support tights which are sold at airport shops, walk about as much as possible, and do the exercises recommended by airlines in their often highly entertaining videos shown around take off time. You could also take an aspirin before a long flight – aspirin thins the blood and so helps prevent clots.

Solar radiation increases dramatically between 30 and 50 thousand feet: so much so that during solar flare storms, airline pilots have been known to reduce their flight paths by 20,000ft to reduce their exposure to radiation. This annoys the airline companies as they're not able to use the jet stream and so save fuel.

Viruses love low humidity cabin air – which, as it is recycled, means one stands a good chance of picking up bugs. Should you wear a mask? There's no need to be too eccentric, but you might try drinking lots of water to prevent dehydration, keep off the booze and the coffee, eat all the fruit and fresh vegetables you can get hold of and you'll be in a better state to fight off infections floating about the cabin.

To fight air sickness, eat small regular meals, never have an empty stomach and you might invest in acupressure wrist-bands.

Ear problems in the air: never fly with a perforated ear drum. Ear ache when flying can be cured by swallowing. To induce swallowing in children, give them something to drink. To counteract ear popping, pinch nostrils and blow hard with mouth closed. Don't worry if you look silly: at least you'll take the minds of nervous flyers off their fears of take off and landing.

*Somebody had to get the tribbles off the Enterprise,
and Lt Sulu drew the short straw.*

May the fleas of a thousand camels infest your armpits!
ARAB CURSE

124 *Number of days it took the ship Gov Morton to sail from New York to
California via the Cape Horn in 1852 (with 108 passengers)*

TRAVEL NOTES

The journey was quite uneventful. The Blue Pacific Rocket was two and a half minutes early at New Orleans, lost four minutes in a tornado over Texas, but flew into a favourable air current at Longitude 95 West, and was able to land at Santa Fe less than forty seconds behind schedule time.

'Forty seconds on a six and a half hour flight. Not so bad,' Lenina conceded.

They slept that night at Santa Fe. The hotel was excellent- incomparably better, for example, than that horrible Aurora Bora palace in which Lenina had suffered so much the previous summer. Liquid air, television, vibro-vacuum massage, radio, boiling caffeine solution, hot contraceptives, and eight different kinds of scent were laid on in every bedroom. The synthetic music plant was working as they entered the hall and left nothing to be desired. A notice in the life announced that there were sixty Escalator-Squash-Racquet Courts in the hotel, and that Obstacle and Electro-magnetic Golf could be played in the park.

'But it sounds simply too lovely,' cried Lenina.

Aldous Huxley, *Brave New World*

DON'T WORRY, THEY SPEAK ENGLISH...

Percentage of English speakers	
Barbados	100%
Belize	65%
Bermuda	95%
Granada	100%
Guiana	75%
Jamaica	97%
Liberia	96%
Montserrat	100%
Nigeria	50%
Papua New Guinea	66%

WHERE IS THE SAFEST PLACE TO SIT ON AN AEROPLANE?

Some say the back is the safest, some say you should try and be far away from the engine. But the short answer is: there is no safest seat. Or at least not one that could be predicted before the accident. The place of impact can be the most important factor, but this is impossible to foresee. In some cases, for example in heavy smoke or fire, the ability to stay calm and remove yourself from the aircraft is much more important than where you are sitting.

The number of dollars the first air stewardesses earned in a month

Lady Jane Digby

Born in Dorset into the aristocratic Digby family in 1807, the notorious and passionate beauty Lady Jane Digby ended her days in Damascus in 1881 as the wife of a Bedouin sheikh. She first married at 17 (the original Cad, the politician Lord Ellenborough), escaped from him to elope to Paris with an Austrian prince, then married a German baron, and had affairs with, among others, the King of Bavaria, a Corfiot count and an Albanian brigand general. She finally found true love and happiness at nearly 50 when she married a Bedouin nobleman 20 years her junior. She divided her time in Syria between the desert where her husband's tribe lived and Damascus where she had a beautiful house in the garden of which she kept a menagerie of exotic beasts. When in Damascus she used to spend some evenings lounging on the roof of the explorer Richard and Isobel Burton's house (he was the British consul in Damascus at the time) smoking a narghile with them and the famous Algerian rebel exile Abd el Kadir who also lived there. She died at Damascus and is buried there, her grave covered by a trim Victorian cross, at her feet a chunk of pink granite, brought her by her husband, from the desert she loved.

INTERNATIONAL EMERGENCY TELEPHONE NUMBERS

	Ambulance	Police
Australia	000	000
France	15	17
Israel	101	100
Jamaica	110	119
Saudi Arabia	997	999
South Africa	10177	101111
Turkey	112	155
USA	911	911
Germany	112	110
Kenya	999	999

QUOTE UNQUOTE

The creation of order, of which man is an example, is realised also in the number of species and habitats, an abundance of landscapes lush and poor. Even deserts and tundras increase the planetary opulence. Curiously, only man and possibly a few birds can appreciate this opulence, being the world's travellers.
PAUL SHEPARD, ecologist

126 *The number, in thousands, of Spaniards who travelled to the UK via tunnels in 2002*

Surviving in the desert

• Remember that it's possible to die of hypothermia during the night in even the hottest of deserts.

• Don't drink too much camel milk as this can be a powerful purgative.

• If you're in the desert and have water, ration it immediately you realise you're lost.

• Water holes are usually marked by large stones or brushwood but beware: these holes tend to be seasonal so are not always available.

• If you can't find water in the desert but can locate a dry stream bed, dig at the lowest point you can find of the outside bend of this stream and you might find water.

• Never dig during the heat of the day because it'll make you sweat more than you're likely to find and you might collapse with heat exhaustion.

• Because of the great extremes of temperature in the desert water condensation using polythene traps can be a good way of gathering water during the night.

• If you have to walk to safety only walk at night: during low night temperatures you can cover as much as 25 miles: if you walk during the day you're unlikely to get further than five miles before collapsing.

• In hot desert temperatures of 40–50°C you need eight pints of water per person per day for healthy kidney function.

• If waiting for rescue, wait in the best shade you can find: under a ground sheet or in the shade of a vehicle and avoid sitting on boiling hot ground.

• To make fires, camel droppings make good fuel.

• Do not strip off your clothes: not only will you burn but you'll lose more water through perspiration than if you keep your clothes on.

• In strong sun, even in temperate countries, always keep your neck and head covered because the brain is very sensitive and cannot tolerate over-heating.

• In both arctic and desert conditions sun glare can cause temporary blindness. If no dark glasses or slitted eyewear (like the sort the Inuit make from bone) are available, smearing soot from a fire below the eye will reduce glare reflected from the skin.

• You could also make a blindfold with slits in it to reduce sand getting blown into the eyes.

SURVIVAL TIPS

Wreckage

If you've managed to escape an air accident, stay by the wreckage as this is where the rescuers will look first.

JUST AROUND THE CORNER

The 'four corners of the Earth' do not quite exist in a geographical reality. However, Cape Horn, at the tip of South America and Cape of Good Hope, at the tip of Africa, have been important navigational 'corners', helping European expansion and expeditions during the Age of Discovery. In religious terms, the 'corners' refer to the 'ends of the world', to which the disciples Paul and John travelled on their biblical missions.

GIVE THE WORLD A BREAK

Safaris and wildlife holidays

In the name of 'conservation', local people often find themselves cleared from their own land and wildlife relentlessly disturbed, so check the area for its sustainable tourism policies.

Off the beaten track?

Don't overly rely on your guidebook, you may end up in backpackers' paradise without having really visited the place. Instead, talk to the locals about their recommendations.

Sex tourism

Many children in South-east Asia are sexually exploited by tourists. There are now laws that prosecute offenders in the UK for crimes committed abroad, so report any unusual behaviour you have witnessed.

Sharing of cultures

Sharing photos and postcards from home is a good way of interacting with people abroad, exposing a bit of your culture in exchange.

Minimise using natural resources

Western travellers' habits are far more wasteful then local peoples and often have damaging effects on the environment, such as excessive water consumption and deforestation. So go easy on your hot showers and other standards.

HIGH-DE-HIGH

The first stories of altitude sickness came from a party led by Diego de Ordas, a conquistador, who climbed the volcano Popocatépetl, 60 miles from modern Mexico city, in 1520. At 5,452m, it was the highest mountain climbed to that date, and remained the highest climbed until the conquests of the first Himalayas.

TRAVEL NOTES

Paris was more familiar to me than any city I had ever known. I had arrived there to study, when I was eighteen, with a copy of George Moore's *Confessions of a Young Man* under my arm. There are certain books that are milestones in my life, and this is one. It gave me the most violent curiosity about Paris. I learned Paris by heart. As I devoured French history, I would go through the streets, book in hand, tracing the houses and palaces in which the people in the history books had lived. I even followed them to their graves in Pere-Lachaise Cemetery or to the king's tombs at St. Denis. Through their books, Madame de Sevigne's and St. Simon's friends were more familiar to me the first winter than my own. I discovered Manet's Olympia hanging amongst the Courbets and Delacroix in the Louvre, which made shivers of excitement run up and down my spine, whether because Olympia was so boldly naked or whether because Manet's painting had excited me, I wasn't sure…

…In the next two summers there were vacationing American college boys with whom to share this curiosity. We discovered Montmartre, and the Lapin Agile with its poetry recitation and cherries in small glasses of brandy. We walked through the narrow streets at night, foolishly unafraid, and we speculated on what went on behind the closed shutters of all the small hotels that lined the streets. We went to the markets at Les Halles where we drank rum in hot milk at dawn, and to the Bals Musettes, where we danced with anyone who asked us – the best dancing of my life. Paris came into my life when I was young, greedy, and energetic and when I had very little real supervision to hamper me.

Memoirs of Bettina Ballard *(former editor of American Vogue)*

WORDS THAT TRAVELLED FAR

Turkey	*kiosk*
Greece	*tonic*
South Africa	*trek*
Greenland	*anorak*
India	*mulligatawny*
Canada	*toboggan*
Czech Republic	*pistol*
Czech Republic	*robot*
Serbo Croatia	*cravat*
Italy	*balcony*
Italy	*banana*
Spain	*cannibal*
Holland	*poppycock*

MAP-MAKING MAGIC

According to Ptolemy, a Greek mathematician and geographer: maps are able to 'exhibit to human understanding... the earth through a portrait'. He drew up a map-makers manual on how to convert the three-dimensional surface of the globe into a two-dimensional map. It was handed down for 1,500 years among map-makers until the Renaissance where it was converted to print, spurring mass circulation.

Gerard Mercator, (1512–1594), an educated geographer living in Antwerp, then the centre of commerce, took this manual to heart and set out to become the 'Prince of modern geographers'. By 1541, he realised the world's largest printed globe, which won him the patronage of Emperor Charles V. Despite brutal incarceration by the Inquisition in 1543 triggering a decade of no production, he managed to produce up to 107 revolutionary maps by the end of his life. He pioneered the systematic use of mathematical grids of longitude and latitude, and the overlapping of adjacent cartographic regions, which seams the entire planet together on a map. He can also boast coining the term 'atlas' after his collection of maps, and pinpointing the magnetic pole.

TRAVEL NOTES

I met a traveller from an antique land
Who said: Two vast and trunkless legs of stone
Stand in the desert... Near them, on the sand,
Half sunk, a shattered visage lies, whose frown,
And wrinkled lip, and sneer of cold command,
Tell that its sculptor well those passions read
Which yet survive, stamped on these lifeless things,
The hand that mocked them, and the heart that fed:
And on the pedestal these words appear:
'My name is Ozymandias, king of kings:
Look on my works, ye Mighty, and despair!'
Nothing beside remains. Round the decay
Of that colossal wreck, boundless and bare
The lone and level sands stretch far away.

Percy Bysshe Shelley, *Ozymandias*

QUOTE UNQUOTE

One of the pleasantest things is going on a journey;
but I like to go by myself.
WILLIAM HAZLITT, essayist

SPANISH LIES

On reaching the Yucatan in 1517, the invading Spaniard Francisco Fernandez de Cordoba asked the Mayan natives what they called the region; they answered 'Yucatan' which meant, in their language, 'I don't understand you'.

Cordoba wasn't the first European to land in this area. A previous expedition of 1511 had been shipwrecked on the coast and the sailors were taken prisoner, so bringing European disease (probably smallpox) to the Mayans which decimated their numbers in waves over the next five years. Cordoba, in fact, was not only looking for conquest, but for slaves to replace the native Cuban population which was already being killed off by European disease and slavery. On landing in the Yucatan, he found a people of sophisticated architects and artisans with whom he traded for gold artifacts before eventually conquering the whole area.

PICTURE THIS

Tips for the amateur travelling photographer:

For dark places use fast film – 400asa and up.

For light places, use slower film, 200 and 100asa.

If photographing into the light, a Polaroid lens will help cut the glare.

A Polaroid lens will also protect your camera's own lens from dust and scratches.

Try not to put film through the x-ray machines at airports – they may claim to be safe...

You can buy x-ray proof bags to keep your film in if you're forced to put it through the machines.

Always keep exposed film in your hand luggage: it's not the end of the world if your dirty laundry's lost in transit, but it's heartbreaking if you loose all the evidence of that wonderful trip of a lifetime.

Take spares: spare batteries, too much film. Better to have too much than to run out of anything on top of Macchu Picchu.

JOURNEY'S END

Percy Bysshe Shelley

Drowned in July 1822, in a boating accident in the Gulf of La Spezia off the coast of Liguria. In the Keats-Shelley house in Rome there's a watercolour of his body being cremated there. His ashes are buried in the Protestant Cemetery in Rome along with his friends Keats and Severn.

FRÜHLING IN WIESBADEN

Henry leant forward for just a second, but it was all it needed to ruin yet another painting.

TRAVEL TEASERS

A man goes for a walk. He walks south one mile, east one mile, and north one mile, and ends up in the same place he started. But that place is not the north pole. Where is it?

Answer on page 153

In Delhi, taxis with black and yellow livery have been the smart way to travel since the design of the Morris Oxford was exported and renamed the Ambassador in 1954. White versions of the same car are still used by Government officials and VIPs.

In London on 24 June 1654 (during Cromwell's Commonwealth), the Court of Aldermen of the City authorised the issue of 200 licences for Hackney Coachmen (no women – following the death of her husband a woman could take over the licence and rent the coach out to another licensed driver – a rule still allowed today).

The word 'Cab' is short for Cabriolet – which means: small, two wheeled, horse-drawn carriage with two seats and a folding hood. A Hansom Cab was one which had the driver standing up behind the enclosed seat where the passenger sat.

The London black cab as we know it was introduced in 1958: with a 2.2 litre diesel engine, automatic gearbox and ability to turn a circle of 25ft (not quite a sixpence) it remained in constant production (with one or two modifications) till 1997 – making it one of the longest lived British motor designs.

To become a taxi driver and the owner of a coveted driver's badge you have to pass 'The Knowledge' – which can take up to four years!

Invented by John Hertz in 1915, the Yellow Cab Co is the oldest largest cab management company in the US. Hertz, a Chicago car dealer, hit upon the idea of starting a cab company when he found he had surplus returned cars when customers traded in their cars. He chose the colour yellow because he read a University of Chicago report that said yellow is the easiest colour to spot. The ubiquitous yellow cab is loved and hated by New Yorkers: loved because it gets you across town more efficiently than the subway; hated because New York's grid-locked traffic is largely contributed to by the 12,053 cabs in circulation.

The word 'Rickshaw' derives from the Japanese expression 'Ji riki' which means 'man powered vehicle'. It's supposed to have been invented in 1870 Japan by an American Missionary, Jonathan Gable, who wanted to provide gainful employment for a poor man he knew. Within 20 years of its invention, the rickshaw was to be seen in such far-lung places as Durban, Simla and Calcutta. And it's still to be seen (usually bicycle-powered) all over the world – from Asia to London, from London to Greenwich Village, New York.

MALARIA – NOT SO TRIVIAL TRIVIA

• Present in 100 countries

• Over 10,000 travellers a year fall ill after their return home from a malarial destination.

• Symptoms can take up to three months to appear.

• Malaria is caused by a Protozoan parasite called *Plasmodium* of which there are four malaria species: *P. vivax, P. falciparum, P. ovale, P. malariae* – all these are carried by the anopheles mosquito which bites mainly at dusk and night time.

• Malaria always takes at least seven days to incubate.

• The most severe Malaria is the one caused by *P. falciparum*. Its symptoms include: fever, headache, chills, muscle weakness, aching, vomiting, cough and diarrhoea and it can well be fatal if not treated within 24 hours of symptoms commencing.

TRAVEL TIPS

Sarongs and pashminas make useful travelling companions. Light, and folded up to practically nothing, they're no bother to carry at the bottom of a day-pack. But should you find yourself wearing shorts but longing to visit a temple where habitual European hot weather semi-nakedness is looked down upon, they make a good skirt. They are also handy as protection from the sun, as a light shawl, a blanket on aeroplanes, an extra pillow or as a bundle in which to tie up loot you've spent the afternoon haggling over in a bazaar.

QUOTE UNQUOTE

When it comes to flying, I am a nervous passenger but a confident drinker and Valium-swallower.
MARTIN AMIS, novelist

DISTINCTIVE DWELLINGS

Treehouses, Hawaii

Want to hush-a-bye baby, on the tree-top? Then the tropical forests of Hawaii are the place to go. The Tree house of the August Moon, on Maui, perches 10ft above the ground in African tulip trees. It has living and sleeping areas, a kitchen, and a balcony complete with hammocks.

There is a flush toilet and hot shower in a separate bamboo 'bathroom', but no electricity.

TRAVEL NOTES

Once the first sense of estrangement is over, the mind finds its surcease in the discovery of the dream-city Alexandria which underpins, underlays the rather commonplace little Mediterranean seaport which it seems, to the uninitiated, to be. It plays even today a somewhat unwilling role as a second capital for Egypt, the only relief offered a resident of Cairo – that burning-glass of a city, wedged between its deserts. It opens upon a dreaming sea and its Homeric waves are rolled and unrolled by the fresh breezes from Rhodes and the Aegean. Going ashore in Alexandria is like walking the plank for instantly you feel, not only the plangently Greek city rising before you, but its backcloth of deserts stretching away into the heart of Africa. It is a place for dramatic partings, irrevocable decisions, last thoughts; everyone feels pushed to the extreme, to the end of his bent. People become monks or nuns or voluptuaries or solitaries without a word of warning. As many people simply disappear as overtly die here. The city does nothing. You hear nothing but the noise of the sea and the echoes of an extraordinary history.

Lawrence Durrell,
from his introduction to EM Forster's guide to Alexandria

Z IS FOR...

Zanzibar, Tanzania
Zion National Park, Utah, US
Zambia
Zürs, Austria
Zakynthos, Greece
Zhejiang, China
Zermatt, Switzerland
Zagora, Morocco
Zamora, Peru
Zennor, Cornwall, England

NOT SO TALL AFTER ALL

Why Everest isn't actually the highest mountain in the world
Many of the thousands of islands in the Pacific Ocean, making up Micronesia and Polynesia, are formed by hot mantle plumes pushing up to the surface from deep in the earth's interior. When they reach the surface they form volcanoes. If these volcanoes are tall enough they stick out above the sea surface to form islands. The tallest of these is Mauna Kea in Hawaii at 4,205m above sea level. If this volcano were measured from its submarine base to its peak, it would be 10,203 m. This is taller than Everest which is only 8,846m!

World's largest peanut

This nutty monolith is a whopping 10ft long and stands atop a 15ft pillar in Ashburn, Georgia. It was erected in 1975 as a memorial to Nora Lawrence Smith, who was a member of the Georgia Journalism Hall of Fame and co-publisher of the *Wiregrass Farmer*. Perhaps she had a passion for peanuts. Or perhaps she just has some very odd relatives.

Spam Museum

Ah spam, that centrepiece of haute cuisine and every child's fantasy food. Previously overlooked, but now celebrated in Austin, Minnesota at the Spam Museum. Thank the lord. Remarkably it is 16,500 square feet and promises to introduce you to the world of spam through videos, fun exhibits and educational games.

Cranberry World

The cranberry is well ingrained in American culture, being as it is the traditional accompaniment to Thanksgiving turkey. And so, to celebrate the berry what better way than to build a museum? Plymouth in Massachusetts obviously had the same thought and so Cranberry World was born. You can learn all about the cranberry and come away ruminating on such facts as: 20% of all cranberries in the US are consumed in the fourth week of November.

Albino Squirrels

Pretty rare, albino squirrels. At least you would have thought. And even rarer, a town claiming to be the sole habitat of such pasty pets. However, there is not one but five towns vying for the honour of being albino squirrel capital of the world. Olney, Illinois; Marionville, Missouri; Kenton, Tennessee; Brevard, North Carolina; and Exeter, Ontario. Each one claims to be the 'real' albino squirrel centre and scoff at the others. And each town has its own slightly strange way of celebrating their pale pets. Olney has a law that gives the squirrels the right of way on the street, and Marionville captures common grey squirrels and throws them out of town.

World's Largest Twine Ball

Darwin in Minnesota has a bit of a soft spot for string. So much so that a resident of the town constructed the largest ever ball of twine. Even though the man who started it all has now gone to the twine ball in the sky, his townspeople keep the tradition going by adding to the ball every year and then celebrating it with a parade and a picnic. It currently weighs almost 8,000kg and has an impressive 12m circumference.

QUOTE UNQUOTE

He who returns from a journey is not the same as he who left.
CHINESE PROVERB

HOTEL ALL THE WAY

'Born in a hotel room – and god damn it → died in a hotel room.'
Eugene O'Neill, (1888–1953) US dramatist. He was born in a
New York City Broadway hotel room. For much of his life he
suffered from a debilitating Parkinson's-like disease. When he died
in 1953, it was – much to his chagrin – also in a hotel room.

TRAVELLING IN DISGUISE

Peter the Great (1672–1725) is best known for engineering a series of reforms that were to put Russia among the major European powers. He was inspired by a two-year incognito Grand Tour of Europe, which he undertook in 1697. Under the name of Peter Mikhailov, he accompanied an embassy to European courts, disguised as a ship's carpenter, seaman, soldier, barber and, to the discomfort of his courtiers, as a dentist. The official purpose of the tour was to meet monarchs and conduct diplomacy, but he succeeded to amass a considerable body of knowledge on western European industrial techniques and state administration. He became determined to modernise the Russian state and to westernise its society. He invited the best European engineers, shipbuilders, architects, craftsmen and merchants to come to Russia and sent hundreds of Russians to Europe to receive the best education. In 1703, he built the new capital of St Petersburg on the recently conquered Gulf of Finland, which enabled access to European sea trade. The 'tsar-reformer' also banned traditional Muscovite dress for all men, introduced military conscription and built the Russian Navy, established technical schools, simplified the alphabet and changed the calendar.

PIECE OF SEAFARING HOGWASH?

The word 'posh' is supposed to have come from the abbreviation on
tickets for P&O journeys between the UK and India back in the days
of Empire. It stood for Port out, Starboard home. The port or left
hand side berths on the way out were in the shade, as were the
starboard or right hand side berths on the way home. To be able to
afford these berths was a sign of wealth and prestige and so posh
became attached to people who weren't afraid of spending a few quid.

However, this explanation has recently come under scrutiny and
some experts believe that the term actually came from the mid 19th
century and originally meant a dandy. The first reference in print
seems to be from a *Punch* cartoon from 1918. This theory is further
supported by P&O denying ever having printed tickets with posh on
and none have ever been found.

The technological parade of welcome: I was already dead with fatigue. Thank you for flying with us today, here is your ticket, change planes in Chicago, you'll have to change planes in Chicago, change in Chicago. They said it so often I began to get the idea I should change planes in Chicago. Change planes: the phrase began to lose any reference to travel; it acquired a dread phenomenological taint. But I did not change those sorts of planes in Chicago. Rather, in Chicago I changed size. For when I deplaned (more tech-talk) I walked into Big People Land.

I was obliged to go a short distance through a glass tube, the story of a life, from one gate to another...

...Airports like abattoirs are white. All this moving meat, these great bodies laughing, phoning, making valuable contacts, astonished me. I was overwhelmed by the size of everything and everybody, their huge bigness! I had to sit down. But where? Everything I sat in dwarfed, engulfed me. I was a baby opossum, writhing in a tablespoon in a Golden Nature Guide. I felt fear, tininess and hunger. I decided the only way to become as big as the Big People was to begin eating.

In the infinite coffee shop, my eyes struggled to take in the polyptych menu and its thousand offerings. Eggs with legs, friendly forks and spoons marched across it. GOOD MORNING! Barnyard suggestions... What! I thought. Wanna meet this chicken in the hayloft in half an hour, fella? But these were not that kind of barnyard suggestion. Here in Big People Land, land-o-lotsa wholesomeness, they were suggesting I eat the following: (1) 3 strips of bacon, 2 pancakes, 2 eggs (any style), 2 sausages, juice, toast and coffee; (2) 6 strips of bacon, 5 pancakes, 4 eggs (any style), 3 sausages, juice, toast and coffee; or (3) 12 strips of bacon, 9 pancakes, 7 eggs (any style), 1.5 gallons of juice, 3 lbs of toast and a 'Bottomless Pit' (which I took to be a typographical error for 'Pot') of coffee. Thus emptying any barnyard I could imagine of all life. Again I was lost. I felt I was visiting Karnak. I pleaded for half an order of toast, eight pieces.

Todd McEwen, *They tell me you are big*

DISTINCTIVE DWELLINGS

Island Palace, Rajasthan, India

With the decline of the old ruling classes, many former palaces and castles have been converted into luxurious hotels. This ornate wonder was built in the 17th century as the summer resort of rulers of the Raj.

It's now a five-star hotel and guests can while away the hours by pools and fountains in cool courtyards, or dine under elegantly-carved white marble arches as the sun sets over the lake.

BRITISH CONSULATES CANNOT...

...get you out of prison
...give legal advice
...get you better treatment in hospital than the locals are given
...investigate a crime
...pay your hotel, legal, or other bills
...pay your travel costs except in exceptional circumstances
...do travel agent's, airline's, bank's or car hire company's jobs
...find you somewhere to live, a job or a work permit

PUDD-ING IT ALL TOGETHER

Flying can be a pesky expense for the enthusiastic traveller who wants to jet around the world. If only flying was free... One man has realised this dream: David Phillips from California has managed to accumulate enough air miles to never have to buy a flight again. But he did not get them in any conventional way. David noticed a promotion on Healthy Choice frozen meals that meant you could claim 500 air miles for every 10 Universal Products bar codes you collected. This got David thinking. He scoured the supermarket and hit gold when he found individual servings of pudding for 25 cents, each with their own barcode. At this point David realised how far this plan could go. He decided to escalate things. He cleaned out the supermarket of pudding. And the warehouse. And then he phoned the distributors of the pudding and found every shop it was in within his area. David visited 10 stores and cleaned them all out of pudding. When he finished he had 12,150 servings of pudding. But then he realised he had only a little time left before the offer ran out and no way of tearing off all the barcodes in time. Not one to give up on an idea, David hit upon the idea of donating all the pudding to a local food bank for the salvation Army who agreed to tear off all the labels in return for the donation. And so he had his barcodes. David sent them all off and hoped that he would not be disqualified on a technicality. Luckily for him the air mile certificates started to pour in, 1,253,000 miles in all. And because he has passed the million mile mark he has also been upgraded to Gold Status, meaning he has a special reservations number, priority booking, upgrades and bonus miles. David has gone down as a cult hero, the man who made good, who saw a loop hole and beat the big guys without breaking the rules. The story was the inspiration behind the 2003 film *Punch Drunk Love* starring Adam Sandler and Emily Watson.

OLD POSTER, NEW CAPTION

Tucson – birthplace of the old 'arrow-through-the-head' gag.

THE SIGNS AREN'T GOOD

Advertisement for donkey rides in Thailand:
Would you like to ride on your own ass?

In a Swiss mountain inn:
Special today – no ice cream.

In a Copenhagen airline ticket office:
We take your bags and send them in all directions.

In a Bangkok temple:
It is forbidden to enter a woman even a foreigner if dressed as a man.

In a Tokyo bar:
Special cocktails for the ladies with nuts.

On the door of a Moscow hotel room:
If this is your first visit to the USSR, you are welcome to it.

In the office of a Roman doctor:
Specialist in women and other diseases.

THE STREETS ARE PAVED WITH... BASALT

The world's oldest paved road is reported to be in Egypt, 43 miles south-west of Cairo. The eight-mile stretch of basalt pavement was built sometime between 2625 and 2250 BC. The road was used to transport blocks of basalt from a quarry to a quay on the now evaporated Lake Moeris. The road was an average of only six feet across and each side of the road was paved with slabs of sandstone and limestone. The basalt was loaded onto barges and carried across the lake to where it joined the River Nile, a connection possible only during the river's annual summer flood. Basalt was an important road material at the time and was used in the construction of many roads. It symbolised the black, organic-rich soil of the Nile flood plain that made Egyptian civilisation possible.

EVER SO HUMBOLDT

Baron von Humboldt (1769–1856) was such an avid explorer that in spite of living through an age when there were excitements at home such as the French Revolution and the age of enlightenment, by the time he died, he had more than 2,000 places: mountains, rivers, ocean currents, even a crater on the moon, named after him.

Humboldt was born in Prussia but spent much of his adult life in his beloved Paris. He travelled through parts of South America, Mexico, North America, Europe and part of Asia. Between 1799 and 1804, he and a French botanist named Bonpland mapped Mexico, Central America and much of South America. These maps were used for years as being the most up to date and relevant ones in existence. It was the first 'modern' scientific exploration of the Amazon region. They explored the River Orinoco and showed that it connected, through the Rio Negro, to the Amazon. They also had to travel 6,400 miles through sweltering, mosquito-infested swamps and jungles, in small hand-paddled boats. This was followed by a trip to the Andes and an attempt to climb Mt.Chimborazo (in Ecuador) then believed to be the tallest mountain in the world. Humboldt held this world high-altitude climbing record for 30 years. While on the west coast of South America, Humboldt noted how the Pacific Ocean runs north along the coast of Peru. That flow was called the Humboldt Current, even though he disclaimed the credit.

As scientist and explorer, Humboldt left his name on the maps of five continents. There is even a moon crater and a lunar sea named after him. Mare Humboldtianum (Humboldt's Sea) is a dark patch of lava filling an ancient impact basin whose extreme eastern floor extends onto the Moon's far-side. The German astronomer Johann Madler named this feature to honour his compatriot, Humboldt. Humboldt's explorations of unfamiliar terrestrial continents in the late 18th and early 19th centuries formed a symbolic analogy to Madler's own lunar surveys, so Mare Humboldtianum represented a physical link between the known and (then) unknown hemispheres of the Moon.

QUOTE UNQUOTE

Whenever I travel I like to keep the seat next to me empty. I found a great way to do it. When someone walks down the aisle and says to you 'Is someone sitting there?' just say, 'no-one except the Lord'.
CAROL LEIFER, comedian

References to Homer's *The Odyssey* in *O Brother Where Art Thou?* (2000)

The names of George Clooney and Holly Hunter's characters (Ulysses and Penelope)

One-eyed Big Dan as the Cyclops (blinded with a burning pole)

The three girls by the river as the Sirens

Ulysses' wife marrying someone else when he comes home

The old-man disguise

The changing of one of Ulysses' companions into an animal

The Baptists as the Lotus-eaters

They catch a ride on a hand-pumped railcar that is being operated by a blind prophet, who tells them that they will not find the treasure they seek. The prophet character in the *The Odyssey* was Teiresias, whom Odysseus consulted in the underworld when he needed information on how to get home again

Odysseus' first encounter upon reaching his home country is with seven sisters (although not his daughters).

Odysseus nearly drowned, but clings to a piece of wood.

Odysseus and Everett both reveal themselves by performing an act no one else could: Odysseus strings a special bow and fires it through seven rings; Everett sings 'Man of Constant Sorrow' as only the leader of the Soggy Bottom Boys can.

Pappy's given name, Menelaus, is the same as the king who declared war on Troy

The Latin equivalent of the Greek name Odysseus is Ulysses.

'Sing in me O Muse...', the line at the beginning of the film, is the first line of *The Odyssey*.

The killing of the cattle of Helios by the 'fools' in *The Odyssey* is mirrored by Baby Face Nelson shooting the cows.

Every time Ulysses falls asleep something bad happens.

The song which plays throughout the movie is called 'Man of Constant Sorrow', Odysseus means 'man who is in constant pain and sorrow'.

Pappy's opposition for Governor's has the first name, Homer

When Ulysses first meets Big Dan in the restaurant, there is a statue of Homer in the background.

The Coen Brothers claim never to have read The Odyssey, *even though the opening titles say that the book is the basis of the film.*

WHEN IN ROME...

Some local taboos and laws it's worth brushing up on:

Turkmenistan: It is illegal to say anything bad about the Turkmen Dictator.

Korea: Triangles are considered a bad omen.

Chile: Avoid an open palm with separated fingers – it means 'stupid'.

China: Handkerchiefs are associated with weeping and funerals.

Japan: Nose blowing in public is not acceptable.

Saudi Arabia: Giving the thumbs up sign is considered very rude and offensive.

Greece, Turkey or Bulgaria: Nodding your head actually means no to some people.

Barbados: It's illegal for anyone, including children, to dress in camouflage clothing.

Fiji, and the Maldives: Topless bathing and nudity is forbidden.

Saudi Arabia: It is illegal for women to drive.

Thailand: You could end up in prison for 15 years if you make critical or defamatory comments about the Royal family.

TRAVEL TEASERS

Rearrange the letters of an African country to
make a South American capital.
Answer on page 153

TRAVELLING IN DISGUISE

Charles II (1630-1685) was intelligent, religiously tolerant and a patron of scientific research and the arts, but somewhat lazy as a ruler, and a hedonistic character. His era is remembered as the time of 'Merry Olde England'. He was forced into exile after the English Civil War. He wandered in disguise in his kingdom for six weeks until he engineered a passage to France, through the isles of Scilly and Jersey. In 1651, he was proclaimed King of Scotland. He returned and invaded England, but was defeated by Cromwell's army. Charles once again fled to France, where he lived a poor existence. He roamed around Germany and the Spanish Netherlands for several years before being invited back to England as the Commonwealth dissolved in 1660. The monarchy, although limited in scope by the strong parliament, was successfully restored. The Tory and Whig Parties were formed during those interregnum years. Charles's reign saw an appalling plague in 1665 and the Great Fire of London in 1666. In 1681, Charles dissolved Parliament for the last time. From henceforth he ruled as an absolute monarch.

The 570 strong group boarding the train at Leicester station thought that they were only going on a good day out. Little did they know that they were taking part in history, as part of Thomas Cook's first excursion in 1841. The trip cost a shilling; children half price.

Thomas Cook brought excursions into the realm of reality: he brought travel for common, ordinary citizens into scope. His approach was revolutionary. He went to Liverpool before taking a group there and checked hotel accommodations and restaurants to ensure that his 350 excursionists had the best possible service. He then wrote *A Handbook of the Trip to Liverpool* in which he gave every detail of the excursion. It was probably the first guidebook of its kind.

Over the years he took tourists to such varied places as: the Paris Exhibition, a 'Grand Circular Tour of Antwerp', Brussels, Waterloo, Cologne, Frankfurt, Heidelberg, Baden Baden and Paris. In 1863, he lead a tour to Paris and Switzerland, and in 1864 to Italy.

In 1865, Cook finally crossed the Atlantic. The first group of European tourists to set foot in America visited among other places: New York, Washington, Niagara, Chicago and the rather gruesome deserted battlefields of Virginia where they saw, 'skulls, arms, and legs all bleaching in the sun.' The party travelled 10,500 miles in nine weeks.

During the famous Nile Tours, there were no hotels built along the route, so in 1868, Cook's trippers travelled as a vast caravan, accompanied by 65 horses, 87 pack mules, tents, beds and field kitchens to prepare Victorian breakfasts of boiled eggs, followed by chicken and cutlets, and dinners of seven courses including wild boar and mutton.

Cook had a bevy of admirers. Oscar Wilde said of Cook: 'They wire money like angels'. Kipling and H Rider Haggard found words of praise. Even the American writer, Mark Twain gave Cook a mention in his writings. Cook's tours not only were for the middle classes, they also attracted the likes of the British Royal Family, The Kaiser, the Czar, many European aristocrats, politicians, bishops, archbishops and more.

The inclusive tour, in which everything is paid for in advance was also a creation of Cook as well as the Circular Note, the forerunner of the traveller's cheque which he created in 1873.

BRITS ON TOUR

Are we a nation of intrepid explorers, following in the footsteps of TE Lawrence and, er, Michael Palin or are we content to holiday at home, ice cream at Whitby and sunburn in Weston-Super-mare? Channel 4 compiled a survey to see where we Brits travelled to in the summer of 2003. And in reverse order, the results are...

20.	Australia	680,000 visitors
19.	New York	885,000
18.	Cruise	940,000
17.	Caribbean	1,015,000
16.	Turkey	1,040,000
15.	The Lake District	1,100,000
14.	Scottish Highlands	1,150,000
13.	Florida	1,250,000
12.	The Algarve	1,260,000
11.	Cyprus	1,338,000
10.	Holiday Centres	1,463,000
9.	North Wales	1,500,000
8.	South Of France	1,850,000
7.	Ireland	2,100,000
6.	Italy	1,294,000
5.	Greek Islands	2,770,000
	Our favourite is Corfu, followed by Crete, then Rhodes	
4.	Balearics	3,811,000
	Majorca is the most popular island and during the summer months, five Brits arrive every single minute	
3.	The Canaries	4,034,000
2.	The Costas	5,877,000
1.	Devon and Cornwall	6,300,000

QUOTE UNQUOTE

Know most of the rooms of thy native country
Before thou goest over the threshold thereof.
THOMAS FULLER, 17th century traveller

FOREIGN PARTS

If you die in Spain or Greece some of your organs may be removed for post mortem purposes – and if they are, they might be retained and not necessarily re-united with your body before repatriation.

OLD POSTER, NEW CAPTION

*It was only on the way down that the tourists realised that the
cable car supports had been designed by Escher.*

DO'S AND DON'TS WHEN
TRAVELLING ABROAD

Do take your shoes off before entering a house in Japan
Don't show the soles of your feet in Nepal
Don't accept the third cup of coffee from a Bedouin
Do shake hands with a Frenchman
Don't stand too close to an Englishman in a queue
Don't come to the point too quickly in Saudi Arabia
Do belch after a good meal in Belgium
Don't eat with your left hand in any country where
you eat from a central dish

The Sanctity of Tribal communities

If determined to visit tribal communities, only do so in the presence of their own guides and do not encourage tourist resorts to exploit traditional rituals for entertainment sake.

Trekking and camping

Misuse of mountain paths, driving off-road, camping outside of sites, littering and building fires disturb both the nature and wildlife, so be mindful when enjoying the beauties nature has to offer.

Bargaining or haggling?

There is a fine line between bargaining and forcing a vendor to actually lose profit out of desperation, so be graceful and remember that your budget is still far greater than theirs.

Endangered species and souvenirs

While no one directly supports poaching, by buying illegal animal products made from the CITES list of endangered species, you are contributing to their disappearance.

Public displays of affection

Body language is interpreted in as many different ways as there are countries, so refrain your self from being overtly affectionate with your partner, friends and locals alike.

QUOTE UNQUOTE

Either this wallpaper goes, or I do.
Famous last words attributed to playwright
OSCAR WILDE in his Paris hotel room.

WHY'S IT CALLED DEATH VALLEY?

In December 1949, a small party of forty-niners wandered into Death Valley when they separated from a larger emigrant group crossing Western Nevada. They hoped they were taking a shortcut to the California gold fields. They managed to get their wagons over the valley floor but couldn't haul them over the Panamint Range in the West. Two scouts were sent to find a way out. The captain of the group explored to the south but died before he reached the waterhole where most of the people waited. The remainder of the party split up. Some people waited for the scouts, who did, eventually, after 26 days exploring, return to guide them out through what's now known as Emigrant Canyon. As they left the valley, a certain Mrs Bennett is said to have looked back and said, 'Goodbye, Death Valley' and the name stuck.

PRETTY FLY FOR A DRUNK GUY

Drinking alcohol while flying is not advised as it dehydrates you. Good advice. Even better advice: don't try and fly a plane when you're drunk. Especially if you're not a pilot. No matter how strong the urge to travel is.

Unfortunately, it was advice unheeded by a 21-year-old Texan man who went on an epic four-day bender and decided, as you do, to fly a plane. He stole one from a hanger in Houston and using the pilot manual, quickly taught himself how to taxi around the runways. Not content with this, he soon took off, but the unavoid-able fact that he was not a pilot caught up with him and he crashed into 100,000 volt electricity lines, causing a huge power cut.

The man emerged unscathed and managed to walk home. However, police soon tracked him to his house. When they questioned him he revealed that he knew the layout of the airport after spending time there completing community service for a previous conviction. Incredulous police also asked him where he was planning on going. He reportedly replied, 'I don't know. Mexico, maybe?'

HOVER AROUND THE WORLD

In 2000, 59-year-old Jennifer Murray made history by being the first woman to circumnavigate the globe in a helicopter. Starting in Surrey, her solo journey over 33 countries took 86 days and spanned 24,000 miles. Jennifer learnt to fly the helicopter in 1994 when her husband bought a helicopter but found he was too busy to learn to fly it.

FAR AND AWAY

The 'remotest human settlement in the world' is the Edinburgh settlement on Tristan Da Cunha island in the southern Atlantic. Its nearest contestant is Port-aux-Francais on the island of Kerguelen in the Indian Ocean – however, despite a few inhabitants, it is principally a research station so it doesn't make the cut.

On the other hand, Tristan Da Cunha is able to sustain its 300 strong population thanks to its delicious crawfish and to collectors around the world who pay top dollar for its rare stamps. The first settlers in the 1800s were from England; hence its native tongue is English. The island now boasts Americans, Europeans and South Africans, who share seven surnames amongst each other.

QUOTE UNQUOTE

Travelling is the ruin of all happiness! There's no looking at a building here after seeing Italy.
FANNY BURNEY, writer

GREAT MIGRATIONS YOU DIDN'T KNOW ABOUT

Lobsters in the Caribbean – walk in lines across the sea floor going to the deep during the hurricane season.

Eels spend about 20 years in European rivers and ponds and are capable of crossing fields at night if it's wet when they begin their great migration returning to the Sargasso Sea in the Caribbean where they were born and where they spawn and die. Their elvers, at about four inches long, set off back to Europe on a marathon two to three year journey, swimming back to Europe at great depths in order to avoid surface currents.

The Arctic Tern flies annually 14,000 miles from the White Sea to Western Australia.

Monarch butterflies fly from Canada to Mexico in huge clouds doing 75 miles (120km) per day.

ARE WE NEARLY THERE YET?

The mile we know and love today originates from the Roman measure of 1,000 (double) paces. It is equivalent to 5,280ft, 1,760 yards or 1,609m. However the mile is not universally defined, its length in yards in different countries:

Norway, *12,182*
Brunswick, *11,816*
Sweden, *11,660*
Hungary, *9,139*
Switzerland, *8,548*
Austria, *8,297*
Prussia, *8,238*
Poland, *8,100*
Italy, *2,025*
England and the United States, *1,760*
Spain, *1,552*
The Netherlands, *1,094*

So, try not to go for a quick five-mile walk in Norway if you want to be back before tea.

TRAVEL TEASERS

Which canal is a backwards God?
Answer on page 153

WORDS THAT TRAVELLED FAR

Alaska	*parka jacket*
Polynesia	*tattoo*
Andes	*poncho*
Caribbean	*barbecue*
San Francisco	*chop suey*
Arabia	*caravan*
Sweden	*ombudsman*
Iceland	*mumps*
Norway	*slalom*
Wales	*penguin*
Wales	*corgi*
Ireland	*whiskey*
Scotland	*slogan*
Turkey	*coffee*

COME FLY WITH ME

To be eligible to join British Airways Cabin Crew, you will need

- To be aged at least 19
- To be a minimum of 5ft 2in in height, with weight in proportion
- To be physically fit
- GCSE (Grade C or above) or equivalent in English and Maths
- The right to live and work within the EU
- Previous customer service experience
- A valid passport allowing unrestricted worldwide travel
- To be fluent in English, and be fluent in a second language OR possess an acceptable relevant qualification
- To live within 45 minutes of the airport at which you are based (usually Heathrow or Gatwick).
- Are prepared to conform to all British Airways Uniform Standards, and have no normally visible tattoos or body piercings.

QUOTE UNQUOTE

*Too often travel, instead of broadening the mind,
merely lengthens the conversation.*
ELIZABETH DREW, journalist and author

DURING THE COMPILATION OF THIS BOOK,
THE COMPANION TEAM...

Spent 327.6 hours daydreaming about exotic locations

Fell asleep on the train home six times and so travelled a little further than intended

Visited seven different countries, and got drunk in six of them

Received 12 postcards from friends and family who were travelling

Stole four towels, and countless bottles of shampoo from hotels

Set off the metal detector at the airport 14 times, 12 times because they forget to take their keys out of their pocket

Purchased 17 useless souvenirs for relatives, eight of them unidentifiable carvings

Worked out they had travelled to an average of 17 countries each and spoke seven languages between them

Spent three hours arguing over who had had the worst ever journey

Lost their passports six times

Found £62.37 of foreign currency lying around the house (£26.88 of which is now obsolete)

Felt guilty about the towels, and posted two of them back

Please note that although every effort has been made to ensure accuracy in this book, the above statistics may be the result of wandering minds.

But why, oh why, do the
wrong people travel,
When the right people stay at home?

Noel Coward

The total number of available seats within the nine aircraft of Air Fiji's fleet, now Fiji's largest domestic carrier

The answers. As if you needed them.

P12.   India

P25.   Montana

P30.   Marco Polo and Mungo Park

P34.   The boy, the older twin, was born on March 1. Then the boat crossed the International Date Line, and the girl was born on February 28. In a leap year, the younger twin celebrates her birthday two days before her older brother.

P42.   Finland

P51.   They were married, whereas everyone else was single.

P58.   Congo

P69.   The Tropic of Capricorn

P76.   Nowhere, you don't bury survivors.

P83.   Minnesota

P93.   As they pass each other, they're both the same distance from New York City, no matter how far each has travelled.

P105. One entered at 7am, the other at 7pm.

P110. 110 miles (73037)

P120. A stamp

P123. Ask one of the men what the other man would answer to the question: 'Is the left road the correct road?' Then assume the answer is false. If the man you ask is the liar, he'll incorrectly give you the truthful man's answer. If the man you ask is the truthful man, he'll correctly give you the liar's wrong answer.

P132. He started one mile north of the latitude in the southern hemisphere that is precisely one mile in circumference. Thus, when he walked the mile east, he went round a complete circle.

P143. MALI – LIMA

P150. SUEZ – ZEUS

Stop worrying about the potholes in the road
and enjoy the journey.

Babs Hoffman

ACKNOWLEDGEMENTS

We gratefully acknowledge permission to reprint extracts of copyright material in this book from the following authors, publishers and executors:

Extract from *Arabian Sands* by Sir Wilfrid Thesiger. Acknowledge Curtis Brown on behalf of The Estate of Sir Wilfrid Thesiger. Copyright © Sir Wilfrid Thesiger (1964)

Extract from *The Gold of California* by Eduardo Galeano by kind permission of Chronicle Books Ltd

Extract from *The Wind in the Willows* by Kenneth Grahame by kind permission of Curtis Brown Group Ltd

Extract from *Kim* by Rudyard Kipling by kind permission of A P Watt Ltd on behalf of the National Trust for Places of Historic Interest or Natural Beauty.

Extract from *In My Fashion* by Bettina Ballard by kind permission of Random House

Extract from *The Rich Bastard's Guide* to Los Angeles by Simon St. Goar Kelton by kind permission of RBG Publishing, www.richbastardsguide.com

Extract from *The Tree Where Man Was Born* by Peter Matthiessen published by The Havill Press. Used by permission of The Random House Group Limited.

Extract from *The Snow Leopard* by Peter Matthiessen published by The Harvill Press. Used by permission of The Random House Group Limited.

Extract from *Journey Into the Mind's Eye* by Lesley Blanch by kind permission of Peters, Fraser & Dunlop

Extract from *The Best of Granta Travel* by Todd McEwen by kind permission of Granta Publications

INDEX

TRAVEL NOTES